Praise

'Talking about music and rhythm makes this book different. *Team Rhythm* is a new approach to management. Congratulations.'

— **Ari Ovaskainen**, Founder at Ovaskainen Consulting

'The mix of concrete content, personal experiences, cartoons (visualisation) and tasks makes *Team Rhythm* exciting and provides fun and variety when you're reading. Thought-provoking impulses stimulate personal reflection and suggest ideas to improve actual situations.'

— **Magda Jackwerth**, Trainee at Vodafone

'The writing style is easy and relaxed, yet precise in content.'

— **Gerald Seggewies**, Agile Coach at Deutsche Telekom

'I enjoyed reading *Team Rhythm* and trying out the exercises.'

— **Harco Smit**, IT Professional, Architecture, Design, Business Process Management, Case Management

'Many of the exercises focus on soft skills, which are often neglected in standard meetings with updates, so these are great to help with team dynamics. I especially like the jazz band analogy as this is what teams can look like – all different sounds and rhythms that together make great music.'

— **Steve Cockerell**, Enterprise Process Architect

'You can find yourself in almost all of the topics in this book – whether as a leader or a member of a team in a small business or corporation, a family or an association. Wherever people come together and work on a common cause, the assistance in this book can lead to a better and faster result. The insights, intentions and experiences from the life of the author are positive, and her request that you have a lot of fun while doing the exercises keeps your curiosity and expectation at a high level. I especially liked the topic on improving listening comprehension.'

— **Andreas Kranz**, Engineer

TEAM
RHYTHM

ELEVEN WAYS TO LEAD YOUR TEAM FROM OVERWHELMED TO INSPIRED

Iris Clermont

R^ethink

With love and appreciation, this book is dedicated
to my three sons, David, Lukas and Christoph, and
to curious and courageous leaders who strive to
improve and empower teams to lead our world to a
better place for current and upcoming generations.

Contents

Foreword

In *Team Rhythm*, Iris Clermont presents a fresh and innovative approach to leadership and behavioural change that will revolutionise the way leaders engage with their teams. Drawing inspiration from music and the power of rhythm, Iris unveils a unique framework that enables leaders to regulate their emotions, break free from old habits and find harmony in their everyday lives. By embracing the metaphorical and literal aspects of rhythm, leaders can create profound connections with their teams, foster trust and cultivate a thriving collaborative environment.

What sets *Team Rhythm* apart is its comprehensive exploration of essential leadership topics. Iris masterfully covers a wide range of areas, including listening skills, conflict resolution, decision-making, diversity and inclusion and more. Through relevant research and her own experiences as an Executive Coach, Iris offers practical strategies and insights that empower leaders to navigate these critical aspects of leadership with confidence and success.

Iris's use of cartoons throughout the book adds a delightful and thought-provoking touch, bringing her ideas and concepts to life with lightness and humour. These illustrations serve as visual reminders of the profound lessons contained within these pages, making the learning experience even more engaging and memorable.

With over twenty-five years of experience working with international teams and organisations in various countries, Iris has a wealth of knowledge to share. Her coaching programmes offer invaluable support for leaders facing the challenges of leading teams through turbulent changes, ensuring sustainable success in key business operations. Through *Team Rhythm*, Iris invites you to embark on a transformative journey of leadership growth, self-discovery and team alignment.

I am confident that *Team Rhythm* will inspire leaders at all levels to embrace the power of rhythm and leverage it to foster authentic connections, unleash their teams' potential and achieve remarkable results. This book is a valuable resource for anyone seeking to create a thriving and harmonious workplace that flourishes at its core. Let the rhythm guide you to new heights of leadership excellence and fulfilment.

Dr Marshall Goldsmith, Thinkers50 #1 Executive Coach and New York Times bestselling author of *The Earned Life, Triggers* and *What Got You Here Won't Get You There*

Introduction

For my clients, middle-management leaders in international telecommunication and medical companies, the pressure of juggling multiple transformations – from organisational and cultural shifts to technical and agile-driven changes – can be overwhelming. It's easy for leaders and their teams to slip into reactive mode, feeling like they're constantly playing catch-up instead of taking the driver's seat. What leaders and teams want is to feel appreciated and contribute to a tangible business impact.

Team Rhythm is for you if you're feeling overburdened, struggling in the eye of a hurricane of transformation. It recognises and supports your strong commitment and willingness to empower and inspire your teams.

From overwhelmed to empowered

One reason that I decided to write my first No 1 Bestseller *Team Magic* and this second book *Team Rhythm* was the inspiration I took from a speech by Mother Teresa, which I listened to when I was a child. In it, Mother Teresa spoke about making our earth a better place, not only by helping the poorest but equally importantly by supporting changing emotional pain in European business worlds to appreciative co-creation.[1] Her words inspired me to improve skills to co-create an environment where leaders and teams can flourish.

Using rhythm and various team-empowering exercises, best practices and visual cartoons, *Team Rhythm* will inspire and enable you to co-create an ongoing or future transformation, making it an easier and more joyful journey for you and your team. Through engagement with the content and rhythm exercises, you will enhance your leadership skills and encourage your team to reach new heights. You can try out all the rhythm exercises without any musical background and explore them for virtual and office teams.

The xylophone model visualises the chapters in *Team Rhythm*, where each tone represents a specific leadership and team development aspect, and clusters them into parts showing the resulting benefits. From the xylophone model, you can choose topics you want to grow and explore more and jump directly into the chapters supporting your leadership needs the most. Alternatively, you can read through the book in a linear way chapter by chapter, starting with strengthening your listening skills in the first part, 'Get Synchronised', working towards continuously empowering your teams and completing at the end of the final chapter with a celebration exercise.

---

1   A Küppers, 'Kempen: Große Momente für neuen Altar (Kempen: Great Moments for a new Altar)', (Westdeutsche Zeitung, 22 November 2009), www.wz.de/nrw/kreis-viersen/kempen-und-grefrath/kempen-grosse-momente-fuer-neuen-altar_aid-31376043, accessed 5 July 2023

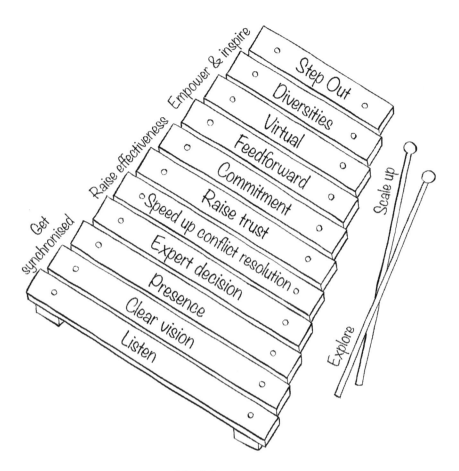

Model xylophone

How and why will we explore musical rhythms in this book? Music is part of our everyday life. We speak in a certain rhythm and melody to enhance our communication. We walk, talk and act in rhythm. Everything we give and take in a team is part of this rhythm. Therefore, we can raise our skills by practising this rhythm to enhance self-awareness and team co-creation.

At the beginning of every chapter, you will find a rhythm exercise. You can practise these exercises alone, in a team or a combination of both. The abstract below shows one of these exercises in its simplest form.

Introduction to the Excel beat format

The notation table is in a familiar Excel format, which gives it the benefit of being accessible to everyone, but this Excel table has a musical twist. With every exercise, you and your team count from one to four at a comfortable tempo. The rows of the table show every one of the four beats as shown above, the image below shows the column that indicates the different accents to play – by 'accents', I mean clapping, stamping, finger-snapping etc – and the circles inside the table show when to play each accent. As you will see later in the book, the dynamic of your playing is represented by the size of the circles.

Almost every exercise consists of an easy version, for those of you with little or no musical experience, and an advanced version, for the musicians on your team. The advanced exercises contain offbeats between the four beats, represented by the word 'and'. When you're exploring these exercises with your virtual teams, I recommend more visual accents like clapping and finger-snapping. For onsite teams, you can use any accents, including your own improvisations.

Different ways of beating, clapping, stamping

You will gain the most from this book and continuously improve your team's inspiration, creativity and efficiency by consulting the key insights and following the way forward at the end of each chapter. These symbols will help to guide you through the book.

The **efficiency best practices symbol** denotes speed-up improvement hints or recommendations to raise efficiency.

Where you see the **empowering team exercise symbol**, you will get additional information about the benefits you and your team will gain, and the duration, number of participants and space you need for each exercise.

The **coaching questions symbol** indicates questions for you to use with your team to enhance thinking beyond horizons or to discover and gain new insights from different perspectives.

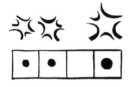

Whenever you see the **rhythm practice symbol**, you will explore and develop the skill from the xylophone related to the chapter together with your team.

After reading and experiencing *Team Rhythm*, you will have clarity about the way forward, exploring your key enablers where you and your team can explicitly see what is worth developing, leading to optimal results for you and your business. I look forward to hearing about your experiences and how your business life changes from being reactive and demand-driven, with never enough time to complete projects or get work done, to creating a team rhythm, so everyone gains and is inspired and engaged. A team rhythm that enables you to create an environment that everyone wishes to be part of. You will have moved from feeling as if you are drowning in a sea of overwhelm to enjoying riding the waves and looking ahead.

I wish you a lot of fun in using these rhythm exercises and insights to strengthen and inspire your team.

PART ONE
Get Synchronised

Achieving synchronisation begins with enhancing listening skills. In today's rapidly evolving world, it's crucial to have a clear vision, strategy and strong leadership presence while continuously developing skills to meet the ever-changing demands of our modern workplace.

Let's start on the journey of getting more synchronised.

1

Raise Your Listening Skills

The first synchronisation step towards aligning with your team and colleagues is to elevate your listening abilities. Speaking less and listening more will enable you as an empowering leader to understand and connect with others on a deeper level. By raising your ability to hear what others are saying, you'll better recognise their needs, desires and goals, and work together towards achieving them.

Active listening skills are crucial in unlocking the wisdom that lies within every person. With these skills, one can gain an enhanced understanding and insight into the experiences of others. Michael Ende's book, *Momo*,[2] emphasises the positive impact of listening deeply to others. The author talks about a person's ability to tune in to the people around them and bring out their deepest knowledge, so everyone can become insightful and inspirational. He uses an example of someone cleaning the floor, concentrating on each sweep of the broom and thereby getting into flow, rather than feeling overwhelmed by the size of the area they have to clean.

---

2   M Ende, *Momo* (Thienemann Verlag, 1973)

I hear similar wise words from project leaders who listen to their teams, focus on a step-by-step approach and improve engagement by celebrating minor successes on the way to value-adding project achievements.

Are you looking to enhance your listening skills and become a better communicator? The rhythm exercise coming up is a light and fun approach that challenges you to listen closely and stay focused. The unique four-layer listening exercise helps you identify your current listening level and provides practical guidance so you can improve. Both practices will unlock your full potential and help you connect with others more effectively.

If you're ready to tune in and start listening, your self-discovery and improvement journey is waiting for you.

TEAM RHYTHM LISTENING PRACTICE

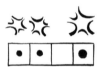 The first rhythm practice will challenge your focus and concentration, and unlock a deeper level of self-awareness. This fun practice demonstrates that becoming and continuously improving as a synchronised team requires training. You experience your actual listening capacity and enhance your listening skills with this rhythm practice.

I recommend you and your team explore this practice in pairs. Each partner chooses and studies one of the rhythms below and avoids looking at the others. It is critical during this exercise to let go of ongoing business challenges and focus on listening to the rhythm.

If you have chosen easy rhythm A, play it twice while your partner listens. They then perform the same rhythm until they feel comfortable with it. Continue playing the rhythm together until you can both repeat it correctly for at least a few loops. Your listening and attentiveness while performing this exercise help you avoid falling into automatism and getting out of sync. Repeating the same cycle helps develop and enhance listening skills.

When you feel comfortable with rhythm A, switch roles. Your partner plays rhythm B while you listen and repeat it.

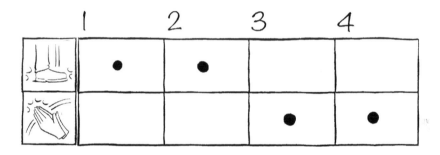

Easy listening rhythm practice A

Easy listening rhythm practice B

Exploring the easy and then the advanced rhythms is a valuable exercise to enhance your listening capabilities. You will notice your mind will learn to bridge the gaps between what people say and what they mean, connect missing dots and create a vivid and coherent picture.

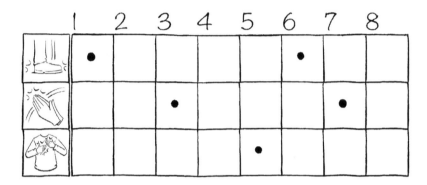

Advanced listening rhythm practice A

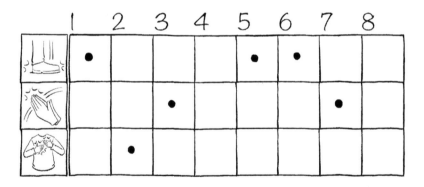

Advanced listening rhythm practice B

What did you notice about your ability to listen and focus on rhythms during this practice? What insights are worth transferring to your daily business?

Exploring listening: What we can gain from bands

To raise your teams' enthusiasm during daily business routines, I want to introduce you to two concrete practices adapted from band workshops. These help musicians become more synchronised via both silence and attentive listening.

During a band performance, imagine everyone is highly self-focused, without noticing the other musicians.

Band members not listening to each other, and the impact

The conductor interrupts the play and encourages the band members to listen to and raise their awareness of the others around them so that they can all repeat the pattern from the other instruments at any moment. The target of this exercise is for everyone in the band to be able to sing or replay the melody, chords and rhythm from any other voice or instrument the next time the conductor interrupts.

Band members listening to each other with applauding audience

Moving their attention from playing their instrument to listening to each other, the musicians open the doors to a new experience. The band grooves as a whole while each member has fun and feels inspired.

The second good practice for a band is conscious silence before they start a new song. Beginning with silence, perhaps a bit longer than usual, raises the attention of all the musicians with the effect that when the song starts, there's a synchronous rhythm from the first to the last pulse.

 What can you as a business leader take from these band practices and merge into your daily routines for your teams and organisation? Paying attention to listening skills supports a great sound and atmosphere, and synchronised rhythm for bands. Transferring this experience to your meeting culture, you can start with a short moment of silence to sharpen your listening skills, leading to inspired teams and applauding customers. Listening means you can repeat your colleagues' words to follow up on what they are saying. Demonstrating authentic listening skills so that everyone can share what they want to add in a meeting without fear of being misunderstood is a significant movement towards a more effective and joyful meeting culture.

FOUR-LAYER LISTENING EXERCISE

Many of us tend to overestimate our abilities when it comes to listening. Have you ever asked yourself, 'Am I as great a listener as I think?' It's a common misconception to believe that we are already great listeners, but the truth is, there's always room for improvement.

Before diving into the best-listening practices in the next section, let's look at the different levels of your listening skills and discover ways to enhance them. This will help you to overcome your blind spots and become more synchronised and connected with others.

Level-0 listening is the fun part of this exercise, where you're allowed to explore interruption. The intention is to discover how it feels when you talk and your colleague constantly interrupts you, and to find out what you are doing when you demonstrate zero-listening behaviour.

Again, this exercise requires you to work in pairs. I want to encourage you to forget your manners. During three impolite minutes, you will constantly interrupt your partner.

Level-0 listening

The key to growing listening skills here is to observe what happens when you walk through the four levels. In level 1, you are silent while noticing your partner's body language or any change in the tone of their voice.

Level-1 listening

Level-2 conversations involve active listening and empathy. This requires you as the listener to be fully present, listen attentively to your partner and respond in a way that shows you understand what they are saying. Reflecting on what your partner has said helps to clarify any misunderstandings and ensure that both parties are on the same page, showing that you are fully engaged in the conversation and actively trying to understand their perspective. Additionally, you're supporting them to the best of your ability, which shows that you are invested in their wellbeing and want to help them in any way possible.

It's important to remember that level-2 conversations are not about you, but rather about actively listening and engaging with your partner. While you may have thoughts or opinions on the topic, it's essential to prioritise your partner's point of view. Overall, level-2 conversations require high emotional intelligence. They create a supportive and productive dialogue that benefits both parties.

Level-2 and -3 listening

Level-3 conversations involve brainstorming potential solutions and weighing the pros and cons of each option. Maintaining a respectful and non-judgemental attitude is vital as you work collaboratively with your colleague towards a mutually agreed-upon solution. The ultimate goal of level-3 conversations is to help your colleague develop insights and strategies for addressing the issue.

Level-3 conversations are entirely focused on assisting your colleague in discovering a solution and generating options for a particular idea or challenge. Giving your undivided attention to the other person and being genuinely curious about their perspective. Both clarifying what is behind a topic and being fully present for your colleague help build trust and understanding. Useful coaching questions include:

- What do you want to achieve related to this topic in three minutes?
- What is your intention?
- What is your idea?
- What could a first step look like?
- What are possible options?
- What is a clever way forward?
- What would an excellent result look like?
- How can I best support you?
- What else is important to share?

Try out these best-practice coaching questions, reflecting on any change in body language or tone of voice. This could help your partner to find more clarity about their chosen topic. I hope you enjoy this exercise and the focus on your colleague's point of view.

Name: Level 0–3 listening skills.

Benefit: Increases listening skills, strengthening effective communications.

Number of participants: Minimum two or in pairs from four to ninety-eight.

Space: A place inside or outside without disturbances, or a virtual room.

Length: Thirty to forty-five minutes.

1. Find someone willing to explore this listening skill exercise with you. Decide on a topic you feel stuck on or that needs to be solved and talk about it with your chosen colleague.

2. Set a timer for three minutes. Explore listening layer 0, then swap roles for the same amount of time. Come back to the next listening level and repeat the process. Finally, reflect using questions from level 3.

Level 0. Constantly interrupt and ignore the words of your partner while focusing only on the topics you have in mind. Look around the room, avoiding eye contact with your colleague. Afterwards, reflect, swap roles and then follow with the next layer.

Level 1. Listen silently throughout the three minutes. This will be challenging if you are someone who loves to talk, but it is worth giving it a try. Notice your partner's body language and listen for any change in their tone of voice. In the reflection period, take special notice of any effect your partner recognised.

Level 2. Focus on your partner. Summarise and reframe what they have said when necessary and react with appropriate body language, eg nodding or smiling.

Level 3. Use your full coaching potential. Include the questions listed earlier and adapt these to your authentic personal leadership style.

3. Reflect on each listening layer with your partner:

- How understood did I feel on a scale from 1 to 10, where 1 means not understood at all and 10 is fully understood?

- How did this conversation improve my situation on a scale from 1 to 10, where 1 means I would have been better off talking to a wall instead and 10 means I know how to resolve my issue with a concrete way forward, actions and life-changing insights?

- How did I feel during each of the three minutes?

4. Complete the exercise by sharing insights with your partner and committing to actions to grow your listening skills to the next level.

Best-listening practices

In this section, you can choose from a collection of powerful active listening questions and adapt them to your authentic wording and language. The aim is to support your colleagues to take time to think and find their own solutions and answers. This helps them step out of their behaviour patterns.

These questions can resolve conflicts as they approach a challenge from a different perspective. They can also assist in a dilemma and move you forward into action. Ultimately, they allow individuals to make decisions and take meaningful steps towards achieving goals. You can use them as a moderator or for your one-to-one personal development conversations.

When your colleagues face challenges and need support in finding solutions to move them forward, these questions help them think through options and identify potential solutions.

- What needs to happen?

- What is unknown?

- What do you think?

- What do you want to achieve?

- What does achieved excellence look like?

- What is in it for you?

- What is the customer and shareholder impact?

- What solutions do you see?

- Who else needs to be involved?

- What do you want to contribute that will not be progressed without you?

- Is there anything else we need to consider that we haven't considered yet?

- What other or better solutions or ideas do you see?

Once your colleague has identified a solution, it's essential to take action and make progress towards achieving the desired outcome. These questions help your colleagues and teams identify the next steps and move towards that action.

- Based on what we have just discussed, where would you like to focus?

- Where do you want to go from here?

- What can you do immediately?

- What's stopping you?

- I understand that you can't see beyond it, but if you were on the other side of the obstacle, what do you imagine you would see from there?

- What is the question I should ask to move you forward?

Whenever your teams or colleagues get stuck in their ways of thinking and need support in looking at things from other perspectives, new viewpoint questions move them into different ways of approaching a situation.

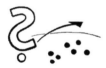

- How true is that?

- What do you mean specifically?

- How do you define 'success'?

- What are the consequences and impacts?

- Which part needs to be clarified?

- Would you like to explore that option and see if it is possible?

- If we take a moment to step out and look at this situation from a distance, what thought comes up for you?

- What advice would you give your best friends if they were in the same position?

- What does your intuition say?

- Since this way is not working, what could you do differently that might work?

- What is most interesting to look at right now?

It's essential to have clarity and transparency around a dilemma or a complex situation. These questions help identify areas where more transparency enables effective decisions and meaningful actions.

- What changes would you like to make in the next x minutes?

- What will be different?

- What priority is this issue for you in your work right now? Top 5, 3 or 1?

- How committed to resolving this are you on a scale of 1–10?

- How motivated are you about resolving this on a scale of 1–10?

- What picture comes to your mind when you think about resolving this?

- What difference would you be able to achieve if you had a team of experts to help you think this through?

Key insights and way forward

Key insights:

- Listening rhythm exercises support your attention growth.

- Exploring listening levels 0–3 shows you where you are with your active listening skills and where there is room for improvement, and how to exercise these skills while having fun.

Way forward:

- Pick your top three layer-3 best-listening questions and adapt them to your unique style.

- Choose three active listening questions and explore the benefits and impact of using them in the coming weeks.

- Notice the gains from the listening exercise in your next onsite or virtual team meeting.

2

Gain From A Clear Vision And Strategy

Welcome to the next part of our journey to team empowerment! I'm grateful for your trust and willingness to work on your leadership skills, which will enhance your abilities and inspire your team.

In this chapter, we'll focus on the second tone of our xylophone model, which represents the importance of a clear vision and strategy. In other words, we are looking at orientating your teams in a definite direction so they can focus on their daily business. When they understand the intention behind your long-term strategies, their effectiveness rises as they make decisions independently. With this knowledge, they can determine the best actions to take to achieve objectives and benefit customers. Whether you're focusing on quality or capturing a specific market, a picture of the business's future situation empowers your teams to effectively realise the optimal scenario picture.

In my leadership coaching sessions, I encourage participants to step back from their daily routines and immerse themselves in nature's beauty. We either take a walk outside and enjoy a stunning view or, if they're lucky enough to be situated in a beauty spot, gaze out from the top floor of their building to take in the breathtaking mountains or the picturesque seascape. Alternatively, we beam ourselves on a peaceful virtual holiday activity, like cycling through the hills, to reflect on the strategic direction of the business and to recharge energy levels.

Let's become clear on your long-term perspective and detach ourselves from the day-to-day operational tasks of your business. In the exercises throughout this chapter, we can practise this approach together. You then gain clarity and vision for your leadership and team's future without being bogged down by short-term issues.

Through the cartoons and exercises, we'll examine the impact of explicit versus unclear strategies and directions. We'll dive into an exercise that explores the effect of a transparent, clear rhythm rather than you as a leader starting a rhythm without any explanation and expecting your teams to follow.

A lack of transparency regarding our vision is similar to driving through fog. It feels as if we are lost as we can't see where we are driving. Heavy fog slows our progress and hinders our ability to move forward effectively. To overcome this, we need to identify where we are and clearly understand our organisation's current situation and any existing dependencies. By doing this, we can remove any roadblocks and gain a clearer view of our direction, which allows us to accelerate our progress towards our goals.

Let's take a practical look at clarifying our direction.

CLEAR VISION RHYTHM PRACTICE

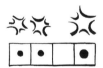

Clarity is vital in this rhythm practice. In daily communication, we need presentation practices to form our vision into explicit and inspiring content so that our audience (our team) listens attentively and understands our message.

You can make your presentation practice fun by using a musical perspective to create a slightly different challenge: how to get rhythms comprehensively understood by your team. The team will not see the rhythm patterns; you describe the beats and present them, but you can ask your audience to confirm a counting-in tempo that's comfortable for them, which helps them to follow and pick up your rhythm speed more quickly.

Easy clear vision rhythm practice

For the advanced exercise, it can be helpful to divide the rhythm into two parts to make it easier to understand: the first bar of 1–4 and the second bar of 1–4, and have the team repeat both separately. Once everyone feels confident with both parts, you can combine the elements, and the leader and the team can try out the whole rhythm.

Advanced clear vision rhythm practice

What did you explore? What helped your team understand, synchronise and repeat the rhythm?

Exploring clarity: From fog to clear vision

Why is it essential to create a clear vision and communicate and share its benefits and intentions with your team? To answer this question and explore the team cartoons with you, I want to share a story from my own life.

I used to live in a tiny village with about 200 inhabitants, surrounded by country roads and small farm tracks. The drive from Munich Airport to this small village was a long and difficult journey at the best of times, but on this particular night, it was made far worse by thick fog. Basically, I couldn't see my hand in front of my face.

As I was driving through this heavy fog, I slowed down as I could hardly see anything. I considered traffic coming in the opposite direction, which is tricky enough to handle on narrow roads even with a good view. As a result, I reduced my speed almost to zero. To calm my fears, I started singing to help me cope in the middle of nowhere with no visibility.

Slow down in foggy conditions

My next concern was how to make sure I arrived home before I fell asleep. How could I speed up in such conditions? How could I do this without endangering myself, other drivers and animals crossing the road?

I was happy when I finally arrived safely in the tiny village, even though it was late. Back home, I reflected on my insights from this drive and adapted them for my business clients.

Speed up with a clear view

When we can't see what's ahead and are unsure of the direction we're travelling, we often feel stuck and lose engagement and innovation. This can happen to both leaders and team members. If the leaders don't know which way to go, the teams will surely be confused about what they're supposed to do.

Missing direction without a clear vision

As you can see from the cartoon above, everybody focuses on their own direction without a clear vision. They are all thinking about themselves and do not support each other. It looks like they are moving slowly or getting stuck and going nowhere.

When a strategy is missing from the information they're given, not communicated clearly, misunderstood or too unrelated to the teams' daily work, it can impact them negatively. Even experts can feel stressed by trying to convince others to follow them, and this means they may not feel appreciated or secure.

Speed up with a clear vision

In this cartoon, the entire team is heading in one direction. The team members are recognised by their leaders and feel engaged enough to move forward to achieve their target while removing any obstacles. When teams I work with have a well-defined purpose and clear direction, I notice a strong sense of alignment, openness to new ideas and understanding of similarities and differences between colleagues. These teams tend to trust each other because they know they are all in the same company boat, rowing in the same direction to win. You don't hear negativity such as 'I'm just a team member' or 'What can I do, I'm only a leader of a tiny group without influence?' Whenever the direction of the organisation is clearly understood and accepted, the teams within it are engaged and empowered to explore obstacles, find solutions and, if necessary, seek help from outside the group.

This next exercise is about getting a more transparent view during the daily turbulence of a middle-management leader's life.

VISION EXERCISE: LOOKING FROM THE FAR DISTANCE

Are you ready to step back and gain a new perspective on your business? This exercise will help you look from a distance and gain clarity on your vision and direction.

Find a natural location outside or look from the top floor of your building if you're lucky enough to have a view of the mountains or sea. Imagine you are on holiday admiring beautiful landscapes. While envisioning or walking to a place where you feel calm, relaxed and far away from your business, imagine one of those lengthy and restful holidays when you can't even remember your passwords when you return to work. Take a slow and deep breath and quieten your thoughts. Allow yourself to simply notice what's around you.

Breathe in and out deeply. In your natural rhythm, notice and enjoy the experience of being here, being connected to the present moment. Your company, management strategy and related benefits are far away. Imagine looking into the distance and seeing your team members as tiny human beings, either gathered together or spread out in different places. Take your time and another couple of deep breaths, enjoying the beautiful wide view in front of your eyes.

What thoughts come up now for an inspiring and responsible leader? What is your wise and empowering message for your team? What will support them with orientation, direction and guiding frameworks that enable them to make and drive their own decisions without the need to check and recheck with you?

For your teams, you are like a ship's captain who can see a bit further with strategic thinking strength. With your clarity and inspiration, you can give them direction, and as a result, significantly empower them. With clear orientation and guidance in place, the experts in your team have the space to explore their creativity and innovation.

Now I want to walk back with you to your team members and explore this follow-up flight exercise with them. This sharpens your direction and ensures they understand your message.

Name: Flight exercise.

Benefit: A light-hearted and fun exercise that ensures your leadership direction is understood by your team members. You openly exchange key messages so you and your team members are better synchronised.

Number of participants: Three to ninety-nine. If eight or more people are involved, I recommend you split into sub-teams and come back together as a group at the end of the exercise, presenting key messages from each sub-team to all of the participants.

Space: Preferably an office space, but offsite. Alternatively, a place inside or outside without disturbances, or a virtual room with the option to split into sub-rooms.

Length: Sixty to ninety minutes.

Imagine you are on a plane heading towards your local airport. You see a couple of other aircraft on their way to the same destination, with your leadership colleagues and their teams on board. You could alternatively use a sailboat or any mode of transport that suits you.

Share your thoughts, impressions and messages for your business situation and direction using this metaphor. Where do you find yourself on your plane? At take-off, above the clouds, during the landing phase? Are you flying right now through the clouds? What is the weather like? Do you have a clear view? Are you faced with fog in front of you? Is there a storm out there or blue sky and sunshine?

What do you want to share with your team and your leadership colleagues piloting the other planes? What is your key message? What are your thoughts about the flight ahead of you?

Conclude by taking insights from your exchanged messages.

Key insights and way forward

Key insights:

- Gain clarity for your vision and business direction via the looking from the far distance exercise.

- Ensure by using the flight exercise that you and your teams are on the same page regarding the organisation's direction. Explore key messages and thoughts from your team.

- Examine the effects on your teams of clarity of direction versus slowing down in confusion with everyone looking in different directions.

Way forward:

- Quarterly, repeat the from the far distance and the pilot exercises to realign your direction for adapted strategies and transformation for your future business successes.

3

Grow Your Leadership Presence

In this third chapter of the 'Get Synchronised' part of the book, we take a deeper look at our leadership presence. As we aim to strengthen our leadership skills and synchronise our efforts within the xylophone model, creating an environment that promotes engagement and connectedness is essential.

By being fully present in the room and utilising our senses to participate actively in meetings and business conversations, we cultivate a sense of calmness and awareness that will positively impact our teams. Our colleagues will notice our engagement and feel more connected, even without us saying a word, leading to a more productive and collaborative work environment. Therefore, investing in constant training to improve our emotional stability and leadership abilities will benefit us and the entire team. By staying grounded and mindful of our intentions and contributions, we naturally train and strengthen our emotional stability and leadership skills, just like we train in the gym to strengthen our muscles.

A good analogy showing the positive effects of presence is a choir singing inside a church. One of many exercises the choir practises to enhance the sound they make is to imagine their voices reaching the people outside the church, perhaps those sitting in the ice cream parlour next door on a late summer's evening. With this image in mind, the singers' bodies move from relaxed to firm, with the right amount of tension needed to fill the room with their presence. The sound will follow. This is lovely to watch and enjoyable to hear. Being surrounded by great music is similar to you being fully present as a leader, filling your team's space with your attention.

Now let's look at the other side of the coin where you are constantly distracted. To illustrate this, let's use the analogy of looking at your smartphone while walking through a park in the dark. Your safety level reduces as you could walk into obstacles or other people, and you might attract thieves and put yourself into a truly dangerous situation.

You can exercise and strengthen your presence skills with meditation, helping to calm yourself down with progressive muscle relaxation exercises, feeling the difference between tension and relaxation and gaining from this realisation in stressful moments when challenges knock at your door. A great resource I have found for doing this is Edmund Jacobson's book, *Progressive Relaxation*.[3] You can train yourself to leave your emotions outside, park them at a chosen location and take them on board when it suits you best.

We will look later in the chapter at the opening exercise for strengthening your leadership presence. For now, let's take a look at an example of salespeople and cashiers in a shop. Imagine attentive personnel who make eye contact and convey via their demeanour that they are here for you and wish to support you with all their expertise and knowledge. This creates a positive customer experience. In contrast, imagine the cashier is busy talking with their friends or is clearly in a bad mood. Compare each scenario to your leadership presence in a meeting room.

---

3   E Jacobson, *Progressive Relaxation* (Third Edition, University of Chicago Press, 1974)

This chapter is about helping you be entirely in the moment, fully present in your mind and body, clear about your intentions and contribution and breathing calmly. We'll look at valuable tools to deal with situations triggered by external factors or individuals and support you in regaining your leadership presence and strength. I hope you get value from exploring this chapter's xylophone tone to grow your leadership presence.

LEADERSHIP PRESENCE RHYTHM PRACTICE

This exercise is an engaging start to strengthening and connecting your energy and presence.

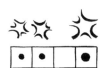 Represent your energy level in a rhythmic flow. One part of the beat is intended to be played quietly, and the second part loudly. The size of the circles represents the loudness, so in this case, the quiet beat needs to be you at your most tranquil and the loud part you at your most exuberant. Try to experience your emotions consciously while playing and listening.

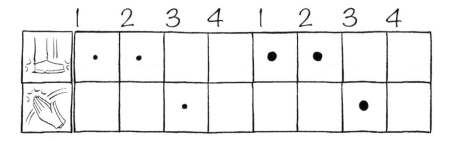

Easy rhythm leadership presence practice

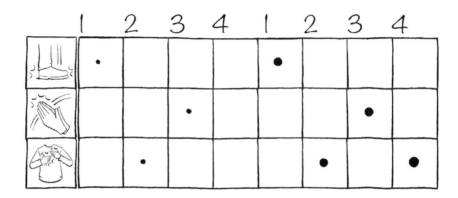

Advanced rhythm leadership presence practice

What did you notice that's worth sharing with your colleagues?

Exploring raising leadership: From distraction to presence

Inspect both cartoons in this section. What are your first impressions?

Observing the first cartoon, we see a distracted and disconnected group. One team member focuses on checking emails. A colleague gazes out the window, wondering what they are doing here. Isn't this just another of too many meetings? They wish they could escape; they would be better off working on their projects. Another person dreams of going on holiday. All the team members' thoughts seem to be wandering elsewhere, outside the room. It's as if they are still awaiting the arrival of a crucial attendee – the leader.

Missing leadership presence causing distraction

In the second cartoon, we see a team fully present in the room with their feet on the ground. They maintain eye contact, demonstrating their awareness of each other. They want to contribute with a clear intention and willingness to support each other.

What they have in common that establishes their connection is their commitment to achieving the desired outcome of the meeting. It is crystal clear to everyone why they're here today, either physically in a meeting room or remotely in a virtual setup. All of them are aware of their strengths and know what they can contribute and add.

Leadership presence adding value

These cartoons show the scenarios in black and white. Our reality is usually somewhere in between, a shade of grey.

What can we gain from the two cartoons? Let's explore a common conference scenario where one leader receives an urgent message and decides to respond to it while simultaneously participating in the meeting. However, multitasking leads to a lack of focus and causes a distraction for the entire group.

Despite many of us having guidelines for effective meetings, similar situations can easily occur in our daily work lives. The solution is to practise leadership presence skills and regularly reflect on our decision-making process. By stepping back from prioritising requests, however urgent, or informing the team about the incoming issue if we do decide to focus on it, we can positively impact the effectiveness of the meeting and contribute more value to the company. Reflecting on the wisest decision from the overall customer and company perspective can guide our actions in these scenarios.

I applaud your commitment to empowering your colleagues by growing your leadership presence. This skill has an essential impact on improved synchronisation.

OPEN-UP EXERCISE

This opening-up exercise can benefit both your business meetings and your get-togethers with your family and friends as it strengthens your relationships. I wish you new insights and business-enhancing experiences, and great success.

Name: Open up.

Benefit: Strengthens your leadership presence for your meetings and supports you in inspiring your teams by discovering the power of opening up your senses and presence in the room. From observing body language to exploring emotions and intentions, you'll gain a new level of empathy and awareness that can improve your communication and relationships.

Number of participants: One.

Space: An office or a virtual room where you can observe your colleagues for ten minutes.

Length: Ten minutes.

Open up your eyes:

What do you see when you're looking at the faces around you? What do you notice when you start smiling? What do you recognise in the faces you see? What do you get out of their expressions?

Open up your ears:

What do you hear? What are the sounds around you? Do you notice any emotions in your colleagues' voices? Is there any vibration in the sound, any pressure? Do you recognise any rhythm? What does it tell you?

Open up your mind:

What do you want to address, focus on and achieve? What are the critical enabling factors in your mind and the minds you are surrounded by? Now is the moment to explore, ask and find out. What is ongoing in your mind? What is your intention? What do you want to contribute here?

Open up your heart:

What do your counterparts want? What emotions are currently in their hearts? What are they feeling here and now? What is your relationship with the colleagues in the office space or virtual room? You can gain tangible transparency by using emojis and writing words expressing the relationship between you and each of your colleagues in this room. What are your insights from this picture?

Open up your body:

Take your time to observe your body language. How does your body feel? What changes do you notice when stretching and relaxing? Look at your feet. Are they standing firmly on the ground? Do you feel safe knowing they are connected to the earth? Where are your arms? How does your backbone feel? Where do you think your centre is? What do you recognise from your colleagues' body language?

Open up your nose:

What do you smell? Does any scent evoke your memories? Does the smell have any effect on you? Is there sufficient fresh air in the room? Would you prefer to change the room's atmosphere?

Open up your mouth:

Before you speak, hold on a second and consider. Is it true, whatever you plan to talk about? Will your words bring value and clarity? Once you're fully present in the room and fully aware of all the colleagues around you and your intention to contribute, this is the time to speak up calmly.

Opening your body makes you aware of the living part of yourself and supports your presence in the room. Opening your heart helps you realise and feel your emotions and heartbeat. Open your mind to recognise what you want to contribute. Your empathy grows with body awareness, attention, compassion and leadership presence.

You can complete this exercise by reflecting on the effect it has on other people's reactions to your contribution compared to previous scenarios when you haven't focused on opening up before speaking.

Key insights and way forward

Key insights:

- Grow your leadership presence while practising the rhythm exercises.

- Raise your leadership presence with the open-up exercise.

- Look carefully at the impact of being distracted versus being fully present.

- Examine the diverse and new perspectives you get from looking at the benefits of leadership presence.

Way forward:

- Incorporate regular presence exercises into your scheduled activities.

PART TWO

Raise Effectiveness

Congratulations! A big round of applause for your leadership development from Part One: 'Get Synchronised', raising your presence and listening skills and giving your team a clear direction. In Part Two, I'd like to share four more tones from the xylophone model, creating space for you to improvise with your team.

This part of our journey starts with raising our effectiveness as leaders by trusting decisions made by the experts in our teams. Even for hierarchical organisations, this is beneficial to overcome slow, bureaucratic processes, empowering our experts to make and drive decisions.

In the second tone of this 'Raise Effectiveness' part of the xylophone, I'm going to share experiences and models to speed up conflict resolution. You'll gain immense benefits from an easy and well-proven working model and best practices to proactively prevent conflicts.

The final two tones on the xylophone for this part focus on growing trust and raising commitment. We'll look deeply into what lies behind the face of trust and participate in exercises to strengthen it, starting to build our team rhythm with an easy commitment and carrying it on with follow-up scaling. Commitment and trust are closely linked like twins and support each other. Trust arises from a commitment to fulfilling and realising promises. As a trustful environment is critical to business success, it is worth exploring.

I hope you gain lots of new ideas and actions, backed up by research and experiences, from the second part of *Team Rhythm*.

4

Raise Effectiveness With Decisions

Welcome to our look at raising effectiveness by deciding to take the fast and high-quality expert-level lane.

How often do you find yourself stuck in endless discussions, going into detail, assessing risks and exploring multiple perspectives and ideas, only to discover that you haven't made any significant progress towards your goal? The fast and efficient expert lane starts with a prototype of an idea, reflecting on the added value of this idea, identifying areas that need improvement and celebrating completed achievements.

Often as an external coach or consultant, I have had to ask the question, 'Who and what is needed to take a decision here?' One root cause of leaders and their teams going around in circles rather than coming to a concrete decision is a lack of basic information. Another is not knowing who is required to make the decision. Especially in hierarchical organisations, consider how much time is wasted in never-ending discussions. Experts recognise their preferred option, but they want a 'go' sign from their leader to be on the safe side. The leader wants to avoid taking responsibility for decision-making to mitigate any risks of comeback. This pattern leads to every decision being passed one level up the hierarchy ladder, which is time- and resource-consuming.

In this chapter, we will look at Frédéric Laloux's organisational pictures from his excellent book *Reinventing Organizations*.[4] This will help us to better understand existing bureaucratic patterns in our business environment and enable the vast hidden speed-up potential that we can easily realise. In the team rhythm practice coming up, we'll compare the effects of the best musicians – representing the experts – in your team taking over the lead and presenting the rhythm versus you as the leader guiding it. I encourage you to do this exercise to gain valuable insights and take action on enabling your team to make decisions at as low a level as possible. I hope you find joy and inspiration from practising it.

DECISION-MAKING AT THE LOWEST LEVEL
RHYTHM PRACTICE

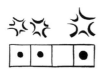

This exercise shows the effect of decision-making at the expert level. The team leader starts playing the rhythm, followed by the person with the most musical experience. What difference do you observe between the leader and the best musician presenting the rhythm? What similar patterns do you notice in your daily business, and what is your conclusion from your reflection?

---

4   F Laloux, *Reinventing Organizations: A guide to creating organizations inspired by the next stage of human consciousness* (Nelson Parker, 2014)

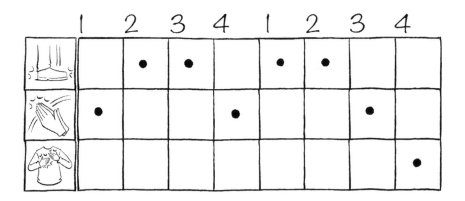

Easy rhythm decision on expert-level practice

Do you have a team member with extensive musical experience in playing a rhythm instrument? In that case, you can gain even more valuable insights by practising the advanced rhythm and paying close attention to the differences between the leader maintaining the rhythm and the musical team member.

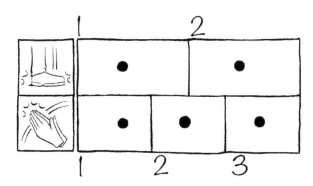

Advanced rhythm decision on expert-level practice

I wish you great new insights.

Exploring decision-making: Speed up at an expert level

The first cartoon shows a self-organising team in which the leader acts in a serving role. When the team members get stuck without finding a solution, they ask the leader for help with ideas, expertise and wisdom.

These leaders trust their teams to take active responsibility for their decisions, thus eradicating bureaucracy and speeding up the decision-making process. As a result of focusing on developing and inspiring individuals, this leader will have a self-reliant team. They can then take breaks and sabbaticals, knowing the empowered team will continue to achieve great results in their absence. Since the leader has pointed them in a well-communicated and -understood direction, the team members know what to do and have room to experiment and prototype their ideas.

Here we see an inspired team supporting and challenging each other to find solutions and overcome obstacles. There is humour and lightness in the room with the freedom to tackle, reflect on and learn from failures.

Speed up effectiveness and efficiency with
decisions made at the lowest possible level

In return for focusing on team growth, a leader will benefit from solution orientation and effective collaboration from their people.

In contrast, the second cartoon shows what happens when leaders decide everything themselves and nobody can satisfy them. Everything comes to a halt when the leader is absent, so they become a bottleneck. The mood among the team swings between frustration, fear and annoyance. Nobody feels comfortable, so no one can contribute their strengths. The team is overwhelmed by various commands that need more clarity, and individuals become even more frustrated when they realise the leader has sent the same request to others in the team. They soon discover and recognise this lack of trust.

One effect we can see in the cartoon is people hiding behind their roles and focusing on passing responsibility on to someone else. Commands are not clearly communicated, so the recipient is left confused and unsure how to respond. They may feel a sense of anxiety and be hesitant to ask for clarification on the intended outcome, going into fight, flight or freeze mode.

Slow down with bureaucracy and a micromanaging leader

This situation can create a toxic environment that does not attract new talent and causes high performers to leave for a more encouraging workplace.

EMPOWERING TEAMS TO DECIDE ON AN EXPERT LEVEL

How can you empower expert team decisions?

It's essential to identify any obstacles that may be hindering your people. When an expert comes to you to make a decision, consider whether the strategy, direction and guidelines of the organisation are fully understood by your teams. Review the exercises and practices from Chapter 2, 'Gain From A Clear Vision And Strategy', to identify clarity gaps until your experts are empowered to make decisions.

Additionally, it's crucial to foster a culture of failure in your organisation, where mistakes are viewed as opportunities for growth and learning. Doing so creates an environment where team members feel comfortable taking the initiative and making decisions independently without constantly relying on their leader. This leads to increased efficiency and effectiveness in the long run.

Frédéric Laloux's book *Reinventing Organizations* uses colour coding for various organisational ways of working, which can be incredibly insightful and enlightening.[5] When I discuss with my clients the different organisational approaches and their colours, such as blue for lean-teal-agile, green for cultural

---

5   F Laloux, *Reinventing Organizations: A guide to creating organizations inspired by the next stage of human consciousness* (Nelson Parker, 2014)

transformation, orange for best practices, amber for military-style hierarchy and red for Mafia-like 'best buddy earns the most', they often recognise themselves as operating each approach on various levels depending on the area of the organisation.

It is fascinating reflecting with teams and organisations on where they see themselves on these levels. On the one hand, some parts of the organisation reflect a hierarchical military culture. Other areas are similar, but support a Mafia-like structure with the ones whose faces fit enjoying the most success. Other departments or teams are already reflecting an adapted agile mindset.

Some organisation leaders have run through and completed a cultural transformation. Here, the orange best practices colour usually appears widely spread across departments. However, I tend to observe a wide split including all the colours and layers rather than a complete green cultural transformation or an entire blue lean-teal-agile organisation.

If you have all the colours represented in your organisation, one major enabler of improving efficiency is ensuring that the experts on your team can make decisions themselves. You can quickly speed up your workflows by trusting your people and embracing the risks of failure. It will happen, but mistakes can also occur with your own middle-management decisions.

A failure culture is essential for enabling your teams to make decisions at the lowest possible level. You can strengthen your failure culture by demonstrating vulnerability and speaking openly with your teams about your failures and learning. Speeding up slow, bureaucratic decision-making processes requires a shift from a cautious, feel-safe mode into a responsible, courageous leading role. Risk-taking and embracing the probability of failure are essential accelerators of a decision-making mindset.

BEST DECISION-DRIVING PRACTICE

 Here, I wish to share my workflow best practices, a helpful template and questions to help you transparently and effectively speed up the decision-making process in your organisation.

These clarification questions are specifically aimed at helping to speed up a decision-making process:

- Who is impacted by this decision?
- Who is an expert in this field it would be wise to involve in the decision-making process?
- Who is the best expert or team to make this decision?

Decision-driving questions to help your organisation gain from initiating innovative ideas more effectively:

- What is missing? What is necessary to allow the expert(s) to come to a decision?
- What needs to be considered?
- Who needs to be informed or consulted to enable the experts to come to the best decisions efficiently?

You can enable fast and effective decision-making by presenting all the options, their potential impacts, benefits and risks in one overall picture.

The template below will help anyone looking to streamline decision-making holistically, including innovative choices from diverse perspectives.

Topic:

Option A

Benefit of option A

Risk or con:

- Risk mitigation – any ideas to minimise the risk?
- Impacted colleagues or customers.

Option B

Benefit of option B

Risk or con:

- Risk mitigation – any ideas to minimise the risk?
- Impacted colleagues or customers.

Option C

Benefit of option C

Risk or con:

- Risk mitigation – any ideas to minimise the risk?
- Impacted colleagues or customers.

Look at this overall picture. Is there anything missing? Does anyone on your team see further options you have not yet considered? Is it worth starting with a minimal viable prototype you can explore, adapt and scale up?

Looking at all your options, benefits, pros and cons, what would your decision look like if you needed to decide here and now?

Questions that support you in speedily realising your decision:

- When is a good time to realise this decision?
- What are your concrete way-forward actions?

Key insights and way forward

Key insights:

- Explore the impact of making decisions at a leadership versus an expert level with this chapter's rhythm practice.

- Making decisions at the lowest possible level can overcome bureaucracy and works even in hierarchical organisations.

- Reflect on where you are with your organisation by looking at Frédéric Laloux's organisational colours, their meanings and your conclusion.

- Get inspired to speed up the decision-making process and drive it forward using best practices.

Way forward:

- Whenever you're feeling frustrated, gain from using best decision practices to get your ideas prototyped and, where successful, scaled up.

- Speed up and spread effective decision-making by empowering your teams to decide autonomously.

- Get inspired by the cartoons in this chapter to further develop yourself and your teams so you can look for even more innovative ideas, continuously improving your business results.

5

Speed Up Conflict Resolution

Welcome to the chapter on conflict resolution. We will explore easily usable communication practices, which prevent conflicts from arising in the first place, and conversational tools to help speed up resolving them when they do arise. We speed up this process by including impacted users, internal customers and stakeholders at an early stage of the resolution.

You may have heard the expression, 'The tone creates the music'. Similarly, even subtle changes in how we speak and interact can have a profound effect on preventing conflict. With a different way of communicating, we can either provoke a conflict and waste time, energy and motivation or avoid conflict from the start. One of our focuses in this chapter will be best practices adapted to everyday business conversations, including communicational research such as conversational intelligence quotient (IQ) from Judith Glaser[6] and violence-free communication from Marshall Rosenberg.[7]

---

6   JE Glaser, *Conversational Intelligence: How great leaders build trust and get extraordinary results* (Routledge, 2016)

7   MB Rosenberg, *Nonviolent Communication: A language of life* (Third Edition, PuddleDancer Press, 2015)

Are you tired of dealing with conflicts that slow down your progress and drain your energy? Do you want to learn new ways to resolve struggles more efficiently and even turn them into opportunities for creativity and innovation? If so, you're in the right place!

In this chapter, we will use fun and engaging exercises to get your rhythm flowing and your mind buzzing with new ideas. We will start with a rhythm exercise that will challenge you to explore disruption in a playful way, experimenting with different beats and speeds to find alignment and harmony. We will also draw inspiration from the blue note in jazz, discovering how conflicts can evolve into powerful expressions of creativity and collaboration. Finally, we will look at the power of an empty paper exercise to help you escape dilemma situations and prevent conflicts before they even start.

Are you ready to embark on this journey? Let's get started and discover the secrets of speeding up conflict resolution!

CONFLICT RESOLUTION RHYTHM PRACTICE

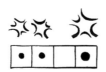

For this exercise, split your team into two groups. Depending on the size of the team, choose about a quarter of the people to be disrupters. These disrupters will play their own beat, as long as it differs from that played by the main group. Allow your disrupters to be confident with their differing beat and play it loud and clear. Their goal is to convince the rest of the team that their beat is the better one.

The rest of the team plays one of the two beats illustrated below and will try not to get distracted by the disrupters and their differing beat. Counting all four beats while they play them is crucial for the main body of your team in this exercise.

The disrupters, however, are free to bring in their own ideas.

Here are some suggestions for your disrupters:

- Play a different tempo.
- Speed up while playing.
- Play a different length of a beat.
- Try different accents.

This exercise should last about two minutes. After that, the disrupters will stop their beat and go with the rest of the team's beat.

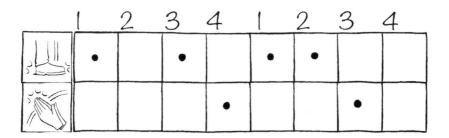

Easy conflict resolution rhythm practice

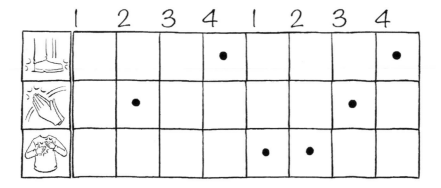

Advanced conflict resolution rhythm practice

> Once you and your team have played the beat all together, you can start giving feedforward (we will cover the concept of feedforward in detail in Chapter 8). What happens when one person tries to disrupt the rest? You can also change roles. In this case, the disrupter becomes part of the team, and a new disrupter is chosen.

Exploring speeding up conflict resolution: Sustaining and holding the blue note

What can we gain from the unique sound of a blue note from a jazz band when we're dealing effectively with conflict in our daily business? Let's see, shall we?

Every jazz band consists of diverse musicians. The lead singer enjoys the spotlight and the applause. Bassists prefer the safety of staying in the background and maintaining a synchronous rhythm for the band together with the drummer. Pianists and those playing instruments such as guitar, saxophone or trombone have the chance to present their abilities with a solo during the performance.

Similarly, diverse teams can take advantage of their differences, giving them the ability to work more efficiently, adding ideas from different perspectives and raising results. Groups of one gender from similar cultural, educational, religious and regional backgrounds with similar values, ages and strengths won't be able to benefit from the positive impacts of diversity.

However, diversities are potential sources of conflict. One essential step in mitigating such disputes is carefully exploring the diversities in your teams and finding resolutions by asking pertinent questions. How can team members best handle conflicts? What works well for this team?

How can the team gain from existing diversities? Where are the individual boundaries each team member wants their colleagues to accept and respect?

Looking into the world of music, we see a similar effect to conflict in dissonance, a note that sounds out of tune with the chord and urges the musician to find a harmonic resolution. This dissonant 'blue note' stands in contradiction to the sound of the other tones of the chord.

Jazz musicians play blue notes deliberately so that the chord can fill the room. The listener ingests the jarring sound and is curious about the improvisation, assuming that each musician in the band is putting all they can – their experience, creativity and ideas – into their part of the music to develop the song to inspire the audience and lead to a standing ovation after the performance.

My observation of teams in business shows similarities to the concept of a blue note. Far from being negative, a jarring conflict shows a solid willingness to add value to the team and company results and successes. Therefore, it is essential to see and appreciate each individual contribution, however much it may jar with 'the way things are done', not least because it provides strong motivation for every team member to be innovative. Once you recognise the potential of conflicts to optimise diverse improvement ideas from different perspectives, you and your teams will find ways to manage conflict to come to an even better solution.

 What can you take from the concept of blue notes as a leader or project manager? What can you incorporate into your daily business routines for your teams and organisations? I hope you will be inspired to create a great sound, atmosphere and synchronised rhythm, leading to motivated teams and applauding customers.

CONFLICT RESOLUTION SPEED-UP METHOD

In my previous business life, working as a proactive international project manager, I woke up every day with various new ideas to improve my projects. At the same time, I was taking care of my three young sons, who are grown up now and starting with their first job experiences. During this time, I permanently crossed my work-life balance borders. I was driving towards getting my ideas realised with my project teams while diverse demands were knocking at my door. I felt overwhelmed and occasionally lost with all these outside demands and challenges.

What helped me develop my skills and become more effective was a programme on how to speed up conflict resolution, making my daily life much easier. Many of the best tools to help speed up conflict resolution were created by Judith Glaser. The one I use the most is her dashboard.[8] This helps conflicting parties to step back and look together from a distance at one clear picture of what's going on, inspiring them to move from distrust to co-creation.

 Often when we observe conflicts, we see the tip of the iceberg and miss the emotional complexity below the surface. The advantage of Judith Glaser's dashboard is that colleagues in conflict are encouraged to look together at the whole picture. Depending on where they think they are, they place dots to represent the emotional challenge they face within a team or with another team. On the left side is a mindset of 'I'm right' and distrust, in the centre is a 'wait and see' mode and on the right is the co-creation area.

8   JE Glaser, *Conversational Intelligence: How great leaders build trust and get extraordinary results* (Routledge, 2016)

Speed up conflict resolution – looking together at the big picture

When looking at all the dots on the left-hand side, we naturally ask, 'How can we get to the right-hand side? What needs to happen?' From this place of questioning, it takes about thirty minutes to find the concrete resolution-orientated actions required to achieve and maintain a more effective right-hand area in future. Instead of blaming others and feeling stressed about proving that we are right and they are wrong, we listen to everyone's perspectives and strive to understand them.

When we work together and trust our colleagues, we can create something new and valuable together. When there is conflict in a group, it can show up as a lot of dots on the left-hand side of the dashboard, so paying attention to and working towards a co-creative resolution where everyone feels heard and respected is essential. With a common look at the dashboard, we can speedily resolve disputes, either between two persons, within a team or between two teams.

It is worth looking at how to speed up conflict resolution or prevent conflicts upfront to raise efficiency.

STARTING WITH AN EMPTY PAGE EXERCISE

Another option to speed up conflict resolution with others when you're faced with too many requests and wondering where to begin is the starting with an empty page exercise. Whenever you can't see the wood for the trees, this is the perfect moment to slow down and sort out some structure. Find your priorities concerning the customer benefit and the shareholder value you can generate with your contribution, and align them in parallel with all of your ongoing private engagements. The best way to start doing this is with a blank piece of paper and a silent moment.

 Name: Start with an empty page.

Benefit: Speed up conflict resolution, raising trust and efficiency.

Number of participants: One.

Space: A room or outside, somewhere you won't get disturbed.

Length: Thirty to forty-five minutes.

1. Look towards the skyline and take a deep breath. Then take a few more deep breaths until you feel relaxed. Once you're relaxed, you're ready to start clustering and structuring activities, requests and ideas.

Consider all ongoing requests coming at you from your leaders, team members or colleagues outside your area. Notice actions initiated by your own ideas, where you are fully engaged in contributing to improving your business environment. Think now about all regular tasks such as scheduled meetings. Look at your calendar.

To get a clear overview, name all these actions and add each one to the category it belongs to. Write it all down on your piece of paper, or in a blank digital document if you prefer. Using colours and awakening your artistic ability can make this task a more joyful experience and raise your creativity. If it is beneficial for you to get a complete view, add all relevant personal engagements to your all-in-one picture.

2. Now it is time to sort and prioritise all the actions on your list. In case prioritising is tricky, you can motivate yourself by looking at the benefits of each one. Consider that if everything on the list is a top priority it means they must all be handled equally and you could end up with everything being the last priority. You will gain from clarity as it helps you get from struggling behind the wave to surfing on top of it. Instead of being driven, you become the driver and make your own decisions. Your colleagues, family and friends also profit as they can rely far more on your commitment to delivering on a promise.

Hints to help you sort out your priorities include adding customer, shareholder and any further benefits next to each action, along with the impacted people. You can write a plus sign for those activities that are easy for you to do and give you energy and inspiration, and a minus sign next to all the actions that you don't enjoy so much. Then give yourself an appreciative pat on the shoulder for your structured all-in-one picture of your schedule, including all your future contributional activities.

3. The next step is to look at this picture and draw a line below the actions you can commit to progressing in the coming day or week. You'll know from years of experience what you can and can't achieve. Decide how much time you'll spend on your daily work, fulfilling your contracted duties; you'll also know how effective you are at the moment. By drawing a line, you can commit to what you are convinced you'll be able to achieve. All topics below this line are visible, and they're valuable to achieve if you find you can do more than you imagined. If you can't, those tasks can wait until you're ready.

4. The next move is to contact all impacted stakeholders, clarifying that your contribution might be delayed, depending on your achieved actions and those below your committed line. This will help to raise your efficiency and trust within the organisation.

5. Finally, take a look at your emotions. When you look at your clear structure with all your prioritised actions, including your committed borderline, how is your stress level on a scale of 1–10? How does that compare to your stress level at the start of the exercise? What has improved for you?

Take good care of your health by changing from chaos to clarity, making decisions and moving towards your chosen destination.

Key insights and way forward

Key insights:

- Solve team conflicts at high speed using this chapter's rhythm exercise.

- Solve team conflicts at high speed using proven conversational tools.

- Gain from conflicts by looking at the impact and beauty of a blue note.

- Reduce stress levels with the empty paper exercise.

Way forward:

- Continue enhancing your conflict resolution skills by proactively engaging and resolving existing conflicts using best practices and methods.

6

Growing Trust

Trust is the foundation of any successful team. It's the glue that holds us together, the solid ground on which we build our relationships and achieve our goals. As a leader in middle management, you likely know how crucial trust is for your team's success, but how do you build it? How do you grow it?

This chapter will inspire you to explore trust in a fun and engaging way using the rhythm exercise. By dividing the beat, clapping and stamping and trusting that you and your team members will land on the correct count, you learn to synchronise and connect with each other on a deeper level.

Why exactly is trust so important? The cartoons in this chapter show us the effect of false assumptions about others' intentions. When we build walls instead of bridges, we create a toxic environment that hinders our progress and stifles our creativity. On the other hand, when we fully trust each other, we create a space where innovation and creativity can unfold in a safe environment. We can rely on each other, support each other and achieve great things together.

The raising trust exercise in this chapter is a powerful tool to build faith and deepen your connections with your team. Exploring the underlying issues preventing you from believing in others can create a culture of openness, collaboration and innovation.

Looking back on my fifteen years of freelancing, I see a bumpy road filled with twists and turns, but what has kept me going is the unwavering belief I have in myself and all the people who cross my path. Knowing that no matter what happens, I can handle it with humour and always make others smile along the way.

I remember hearing a speech by Mother Teresa about her intention to make people feel better, which has stayed with me ever since. She reminded me that each moment is the most important moment of our lives, and the person we are with right now is the most important. It's inspirational to approach each person we meet with trust and appreciation.

In this chapter, we'll dive deep into what we find behind trust and show how to grow it with the trust-raising exercise. Let's get started and discover the power of trust together!

TRUST RHYTHM PRACTICE

In a musical context, trust is an integral part of band members playing together. The overall sound only works when everybody plays in harmony with each other, the rhythm maintains a beat or groove and the band fuses in every aspect.

 This practice will drive you to find trust in rhythm. In the process, the rhythm accents will be separated, so divide your team into two groups. The first will play the stomp accent, and the second the clap accent.

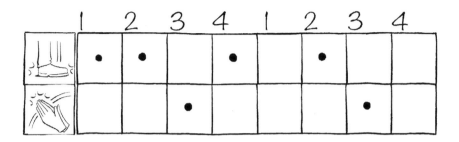

Easy trust rhythm practice

Depending on your preference, for the advanced exercise, your team can be split into two or four groups. If you decide on two groups, each group plays two of the four accents. During this exercise, everyone on your team can find their strengths and bring them into practice. Moreover, you will all pay attention to each other and learn that the beat will continue even when one of you forgets to play an accent or plays at the wrong time.

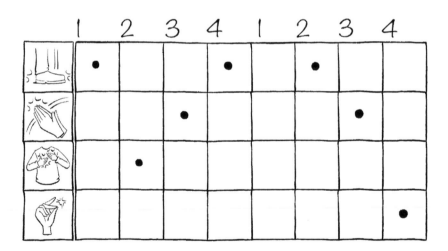

Advanced trust rhythm practice

Use this practice to strengthen your ability to show vulnerability and generosity, noticing the impact of failures.

Instead of the whole team stopping when you or someone else loses the beat, you learn to carry on with faith in your team's strengths.

Exploring distrust to trust

Look at the first cartoon. What do you see? What is your impression?

Impact of distrust

The leader in the first cartoon is looking at a vast stone wall. He is trapped in a cage, feeling like a prisoner while holding the keys to escape. On the other side of the wall, the team wonders about the barrier between them and what is going on in the leader's mind. What prevents him from engaging with them? From the leader's perspective, he is convinced he cannot trust this team. He even doubts if he can trust himself.

Various thoughts appear in his mind. 'Most of the people in my team are lazy, and some need help to perform their tasks. They never, ever do what I want and need from them. If I were not here, nothing would work, and we would not get anything done to the quality I am looking for. What do they think about me? I am sure they want to get rid of me, and as soon as I turn my back, they take the easy route rather than the route I have in mind, which is the best one.' His thoughts go on and on like a bad movie, examining all worst-case scenarios in detail.

These beliefs are probably wrong, and they're definitely blocking and harming the leader from getting the best from his people. After all, none of us knows what is really going on in the minds of others; most of the time, we don't even know the truth behind our behaviours and stories. In this space of distrust, we risk hindering collaboration and avoiding creativity. Keep in mind that we have only one life. It's our choice whether we trust or distrust.

Let's have a look now at another cartoon.

Gain from trust

The team in this cartoon is co-creating. Everyone in the team is full of energy, inspired and motivated. There are no hidden assumptions, no hidden agendas. They fully trust each other.

We can see in this second cartoon what happens in a trustful environment. The team members are having fun. They observe and solve problems together, removing obstacles that are hindering progress even when something unexpected or unintended occurs. They believe their colleagues have the best intentions to contribute and add value to the team. This team will easily attract new talent.

 With this belief and trust in one another in mind, team members naturally communicate in a supportive way, asking each other:

- How can we help each other?

- How can we solve this issue together?

- What is needed?

- Do we need to clarify our direction?

- Is there any expertise on the team that can benefit us?

Here, we are far away from a blame culture. No matter what happens, even when we face many changes, transformations and demands, trust gives us the grounding and foundation to act in an inspiring team atmosphere.

A valuable takeaway for leaders from these pictures is the different impacts of trusting or distrusting our teams. Take a moment to look once again at both cartoons.

 Where do you see yourself in terms of trust? What is your conclusion?

As you probably know, trust doesn't grow overnight; it requires attention.
It takes time and effort to develop, so taking a deeper look at what
it means can be valuable. We can strengthen our ability to believe in
ourselves and others by practising the trust exercise coming up. First,
though, a story from my own life that leads us into what is behind trust.

DEEP DIVE INTO WHAT YOU FIND BEHIND TRUST

I want to share the beginnings of my fifteen-year freelancing
celebration with you. I hope it will bring a smile to your face.

At the time of my most significant life-changing moment, I'd
worked for seventeen years as an international consultant and
project manager in the telecom industry. I liked my job and
enjoyed the interesting worldwide projects, but I worked quite
a lot, which didn't change when I stepped from employment
to freelancing. What did change was that I switched from
a secure, exciting, fulfilling project manager and business
consultant job to something altogether more insecure. I did
this because I felt I was missing out on:

- Being able to follow my strategy

- Seeing the effect of my contribution

- Working without a safety net

- Trusting in my skills and expertise

- Having the ability to grow, learn and choose my own
  strategic directions

I remember the moment I decided to move from the safety of
being an international company employee to restarting as an
independent freelancer. I was on a one-week retreat on a small
island, walking around it surrounded by the sea. The road was

coming to a fork, one route going to the right and the other to the left. I wanted to know which route I should take for my life, so I chose the smaller and narrower path in front of me. As I made my decision and walked without hesitation along the path, I felt trust coming from inside, remembering that I could always change my mind and make a different choice.

If we notice something is going wrong, we can always choose again and redirect ourselves or even turn around. It's standing still and doing nothing that keeps us stuck and driven by others.

I needed courage and trust to move forward into an unknown business life while my three sons were still in school. Reflecting on my years of experience and basing my new venture on all the projects I'd completed and the business connections I'd made, I felt more like I was crossing a bridge to face the uncertainties and challenges in front of me rather than jumping into the cold water below. Thanks to the confidence I'd gained from my seventeen years of valuable experience, I could happily take my first step to explore a new path.

As I continued along the new path, my faith in myself and those around me grew with each step. On my first day as a freelancer, I took a walk through the woods. I felt free as I realised that I could design my own strategy, take risks and be responsible for my future success. I was full of energy and it was as if the sky above the green woods was opening up along with all the opportunities that awaited me.

During the last fifteen years, I've had the chance to look deeper below the surface of trust with research and experiences. Believing in others is a critical ingredient in building an empowered, high-performing team. Creating a transparent and open communication culture is essential to generate trust, where team members can feel safe to share their thoughts, feelings and ideas without fear of judgement. It then becomes easier to learn from failures and move forward, giving you and your team space for open and honest communication and sharing intentions.

Listening to connect and expressing needs, interests and aspirations is essential in this communication culture to deepen relationships within the team. Trust in each other's intentions is critical, as is you as a leader acting as a role model for high ethical standards. It's also crucial for you and all team members to respect each other's opinions and appreciate each other's ideas, recognising that this respect leads to more creativity and better results.

By speaking openly about our intentions and the resulting benefits, along with our emotions, we establish deeper connections with our colleagues and create a shared vision for success. Looking for opposite and varying viewpoints and clarifying what success looks like for our colleagues helps build a culture of mutual respect and trust.

 Key questions and statements supporting trust are:

- What do you think?
- What ideas are coming up for you?
- Can you draw a picture of a future success scenario you have in your mind?
- What is the intention behind this scenario?
- Do you see anything else?
- What is worth sharing?

- I highly appreciate your ideas, your thoughts and your perspective.

It's helpful to regularly reflect on our actions and behaviours as leaders, asking questions such as 'How often do I ask open team-empowering questions?', 'How often do I appreciate ideas and unique strengths that contribute to the team's effectiveness or identity?' or 'How often do I demonstrate vulnerability by sharing failures and learnings?'

Understanding is also crucial to building trust. Investing time looking for more options and ideas, stepping into our colleagues' shoes and experiencing their perspective raises this understanding. Whenever we and our colleagues come to agreements while remaining aware that nobody is perfect, we strengthen our trust level in our team. By asking questions and drawing pictures to ensure everyone is on the same page, we can create a shared understanding of what success looks like and align our efforts towards achieving it. I highly recommend listening to the song 'Not Perfect' by Tim Minchin to strengthen your big-picture perspective and lighten perfectionism with a portion of musical humour.

Finally, validation of existing assumptions and reviewing their absolute truth is vital to building trust as it allows us to adapt our beliefs based on facts. Speaking up when something feels or sounds wrong and sharing various future success scenarios, including ideas from the whole team, keeps communication solution-orientated. This can only help to grow our co-creation culture.

RAISING TRUST EXERCISE

This exercise is helpful whenever you notice there's a need in your team for more understanding of other people's perspectives. It's also helpful to resolve ongoing conflicts, especially when team members are gossiping behind each other's backs rather than openly speaking about what needs to change. This exercise allows you to reflect on and improve the current and similar future situations, which will inevitably raise trust within your team.

Name: Raising trust.

Benefit: Proactive conflict resolution and raising trust and understanding, strengthened by the ability to challenge your own beliefs and assumptions.

Number of participants: Two or a group divided into pairs.

Space: Ideally, a room inside or an area outside with as few disturbances as possible so you and your partner or team can focus on the exercise.

Length: Thirty to sixty minutes, depending on the complexity of the scenario you want to use as an example and the number of people involved.

1. Choose a situation from your experience that wasn't going in the best direction. A time you missed a chance to speak up when you perceived something was wrong and contrary to your values is perfect for this exercise.

2. Share your story from your perspective with your partner.

3. Change your point of view. Put yourself in the shoes of the other people involved. Tell the same story from their perspective and memory. Move around the space of your scenario from person to person.

4. Imagine there's a camera in the room, watching the scenario from an unbiased and objective point of view. A camera cannot feel, assume or interpret; it just records words, tone of voice, mimicry and gestures. Take care that you tell the story from this neutral perspective without jumping back into emotions or interpretations.

5. Now it's time to swap so the listener can share and explore your story from diverse viewpoints.

6. Reflect on what you have noticed from looking at this scenario from all the different perspectives. What has changed for you? What changes did you notice as a listener and observer in your partner's tone of voice, body language, mimicry and usage of words?

This exercise uncovers the hidden obstacles preventing you from realising better team achievements with more clarity.

Key insights and way forward

Key insights:

- Learn to trust that your team will be able to keep the rhythm even if one of you misses a beat.

- The cartoon teams in this chapter give you ideas on how to grow trust, observing the impact of trust versus distrust.

- Unblock trust areas by deep diving into what there is behind them.

- Raise confidence in your colleagues and teams by exploring a scenario from all the involved participants' perspectives.

Way forward:

- Continuously grow your team's trust levels with this chapter's exercises.

- Share your intentions openly whenever appropriate.

- Speak up whenever you feel something is going wrong, painting a picture of future team achievements and benefits.

7

Start With An Easy Commitment And Scale Up

Welcome to the chapter on commitment, the twin of trust. Here, we will explore the impact of zero commitment versus the benefits of complete commitment.

To illustrate this impact, this chapter's cartoons start with a choir showing zero commitment. The singers show up whenever they want. Some forget their notes, while others do not practise at all or focus on the wrong songs. A choir that lacks commitment has a negative impact on the concert experience. This leads to a disappointing musical performance, leaving the audience dissatisfied with the overall nightmare of a sound.

On the other hand, when a choir has a high level of commitment (ten out of ten), each musician strives to continuously develop their musical skills. They work together to optimise their performance, taking feedforward and suggestions from each other. The result is a great sound that touches the audience's hearts, leading to a standing ovation.

In the commitment exercise, we'll explore how collecting feedforward from each other can have a positive impact. We'll start with a simple commitment to concrete action, focusing on the benefits of following through on this commitment to keep things light and enjoyable.

To increase the likelihood of us sticking to our commitments, we'll examine what will help us stay on track beforehand. By sharing our successes and co-creating solutions for any obstacles that may arise, we can work together to overcome challenges. As we saw in the previous chapter, it's important to recognise that we are not perfect, and that's OK. A culture of trust encourages vulnerability as a natural part of the learning process and allows us to embrace failure as an opportunity for growth.

We will examine how agile teams learn and grow by reflecting on their commitment. This includes improving their reliability and making more realistic plans based on past experiences. In my experience, agile teams tend to be optimistic to start with, but often only complete half of what they intended to achieve. However, they then become more realistic about what they can accomplish, which helps them synchronise better with the teams they depend on. This shows that commitment can increase over time with practice and experience.

Trust and commitment are vital in any organisation, but especially in international companies where various teams and departments collaborate and depend on each other's results. These teams must be open and honest about what they can and cannot achieve, and sometimes people need to say no to be able to keep promises. We can learn from agile teams who prioritise and focus on the most critical tasks and show transparency about the backlogs they do not commit to clearing. This transparency leads to reliability and enables teams to count on each other, with the effect that everyone has more fun and raises effectiveness and efficiency.

Commitment may not sound beautiful or joyful at first, but when you look into the smiling face of the one who benefits from your reliability, you realise its beauty. Let's strive to commit to commitment. We'll soon wonder why others act any differently.

In this rhythm exercise, we explore another side of commitment: the effect of setting accents as a metaphor for transparency in our business journey.

COMMITMENT RHYTHM PRACTICE

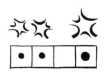 Commitment consists of explicit statements. In a rhythmic language, this means clear accents. Playing a loud, strong accent (in our practice with beats one and three), we will bring orientation to the listener. Accent one is especially crucial because it marks the beginning of the communication. When you don't play the first accent or play it too softly, you and the listener will miss the chance to get synchronised.

So you can explore the difference, this practice is separated into a clear and unclear rhythm. First, one person will play the beat with clear accents, and then use the inaccurate version.

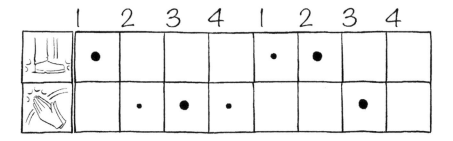

Clear commitment rhythm practice

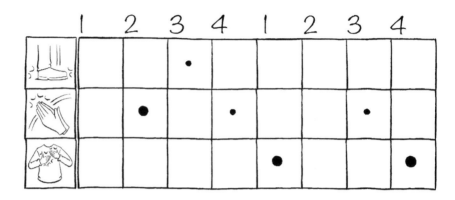

Unclear commitment rhythm practice

The listening team shares their impressions of each rhythm and reflects on similarities to business situations. Just like the size of the circles in the cartoons indicates the volume of the sound, remember that even minor actions or words can significantly impact those around us. Let's strive to make every interaction count, whether big or small.

Exploring the commitment effect from zero to ten

Imagine there is zero commitment in a business team. How could this look? Everyone focuses solely on their benefits and how to advance themselves, whether through pursuing bonuses or promotions, gaining more power over others or exploring their creative ideas without involving others.

Unfortunately, this behaviour leads to team members overlooking essential factors such as company strategy and customer needs. They pick up and drop their job-related actions whenever they feel like it. When asked to do something, they typically respond with maybe, which shows zero commitment.

For their part, the leader shares a message with the team, and a moment later, changes the strategic direction as they regard something else as suddenly having become more critical. Crucially, though, they forget to tell the team about the change of direction and intention. What a chaotic mess! Would you like to be part of such a team? Would you trust this team to achieve valuable results for customers and help the company survive in the market? Personally, I'd rather not.

What would a team with a commitment level of ten look like? What positive changes would your team experience if you encouraged them to raise their commitment level by just one point? Let's look at the different impacts from a musical perspective. In the first scenario, a choir has a commitment level of zero, leading to people in the audience leaving the concert fast, disappointed, angry and frustrated.

Choir with a commitment level of zero in concert

In the second cartoon, the choir has a commitment level of ten. The audience enjoys the beautiful synchronised sound and responds at the end of the concert with a standing ovation.

Choir that has raised its commitment level to ten in concert

 What valuable business insights or personal reflections did you gain from exploring the different impacts of a zero versus a ten commitment?

COMMITMENT EXPLORATION AND UPSCALING EXERCISE

While this commitment exercise is short, easy and light, it has a substantial empowering effect on any team workshop. Are you ready to take your team's creativity, inspiration and engagement to the next level?

Imagine the powerful impact of each individual on your team committing to a small, easy-to-do action during your next workshop or team event. When you reflect on the resulting benefits afterwards, you'll see how these small individual commitments led to significant team transformations. Let's look at these tiny improvement initiatives and see how far they can take you.

Name: Starting with a simple commitment.

Benefit: Raise efficiency and become more reliable.

Number of participants: Three to twenty.

Space: A room, a space outside or a virtual room, wherever your offsite or retrospective meetings take place.

Length: Ten to twenty minutes.

1. What can each of the participants do to become even more effective and creative, and gain more ideas? Imagine the effect of your commitment action contributing to the success and positivity of the workshop. What contribution fits this workshop team best?

2. To get some ideas, choose from and adapt these options:

- Listening to what my colleagues intend to say before responding.

- Asking my leaders and colleagues for their ideas.

- Being fully present in the room.

- Showing clarity by sharing my intentions.

- Taking care to stay focused.

- Speaking up whenever I feel something is going in the wrong direction, reminding others of the aim of the workshop and asking what the best route is right now. What should we focus on?

When you feel triggered and your natural response is to freeze, fight or flee, shift your focus towards contributing to the workshop's results. You can do this by asking yourself, 'How can I share my thoughts on the high-level scenario we are aiming for?' This simple question helps you stay engaged in the conversation and keeps the discussion moving forward towards a productive outcome.

Even better, create your best-fit commitments.

3. In pairs, share your commitment with a partner. You get a minimum of two minutes each, but consider taking a bit more time during this part and perhaps having a short walk outside. Challenge your partner by asking:

- What is the concrete action related to your commitment?

- Can you start with a more accessible, fun activity to create an enjoyable experience?

- What could help you to realise your committed action?

- What benefit do you intend to realise from your committed contribution?

4. Share your partner's commitment action and intended benefit with the rest of the group.

5. Complete by scaling the realisation of your committed contribution from 1 to 10, where 1 means you forgot about your action and 10 means you realised your commitment and can see the gain. Share the differences you notice from this commitment practice.

6. Take a look at upscaling options from your commitment experience. Which of your actions are easy to do and worth transferring into your daily business? What added value that you observed from your commitment action is it beneficial to expand? What do your adapted and enhanced activities for your daily business look like, and what do you expect to gain? When and where is a good time to refresh your commitments?

I'd be interested to hear about your experiences with the commitment exercise and how they have impacted your team's reliability.

SUCCEED IN RAISING RELIABILITY USING A DEFINITION OF EXCELLENCE

What can we learn from agile teams concerning commitments? They become increasingly reliable, learning from experiences and committing to actions. What helps them to keep promises is being transparent about value-adding activities for leaders, users and customers. This transparency enables teams to welcome changes even late in a process.

Committing to accessible prototypes presenting minimal viable products to users and customers makes it easier to adapt these products at an early stage. This commitment leads to beneficial effects for involved production teams, sales colleagues and clients who all gain from good prognoses and forecasts.

Let's transfer the success secrets from agile teams to keeping your commitments and improving synchronisation in your environment. Here, we'll explore powerful questions that can help you stay focused and deliver on your promises.

What do you want to demonstrate a week from now to your internal and external customers? How would your planned results look if you intended to show them excellent achievements so they can see what is in it for them? What would cause tumultuous applause and huge smiles?

 Let's take a moment to reflect on the past two weeks and set clear goals for the week ahead. What did you accomplish during this time? Was there a particularly challenging workload that won't be repeated? Based on your experience, what can you realistically commit to achieving? By presenting an executive summary or elevator speech to deliver at the end of the coming week, you can demonstrate to your customers and colleagues that you are committed and they can count on you and your team.

These are similar to agile team questions but adapted to a leader's daily routine. They show you see a benefit in raising your reliability and commitment levels so people around you can happily trust you.

Key insights and way forward

Key insights:

- Starting a workshop with a commitment has a substantial positive impact on the outcomes and atmosphere.

- Raising our reliability leads to trust and effectively synchronises business outcomes.

- From the rhythm accents exercise, we learn that even the smallest actions or words can have a big impact.

- Looking at a choir with and without commitment, we can see how the audience reacts differently.

Way forward:

- Try the commitment exploration and upscaling exercise in your next workshop with your team. You are more than welcome to share the results with me.

- Keep on challenging yourself, scaling up your commitments in both your professional and personal life, and becoming a more trusted and reliable leader that others can count on.

PART THREE
Continuously Empower And Inspire Your Teams

As we approach the final stage of our journey towards continuous empowerment and inspiration of our teams, it's important to focus on regular improvements through the use of feedforward, embracing diversity and harnessing its creative potential. While we know that diverse teams lead to better results, it is beneficial to be mindful of the unique challenges of working in such an environment as we strive towards further diversifying our teams.

To expand our horizons, we can look beyond our business areas and draw inspiration from sources such as musical bands, film productions and software development teams, even though they may not be directly related to our industry. Finally, we will celebrate our achievements with the concluding *Team Rhythm* exercise as we reach the end of our journey together. I wish you success and new inspiration as you explore these empowering team exercises, and hope you take fun and insights from the cartoons and best practices, inspiring you in your daily business and beyond.

8

Add More Value Via Feedforward

Welcome to the chapter on discovering the power of feedforward, a concept championed by leadership coach and author Marshall Goldsmith.[9] In this chapter, we will explore how to unlock your true potential, gain new insights and identify areas for growth by seeking feedforward from your colleagues. By having the courage to be open to new ideas and perspectives, you can discover your strengths and blind spots and make positive changes to enhance your daily business.

In my previous leadership job, feedforward was one major time efficiency enabler for me. My colleagues greatly appreciated my regular feedforward about my strengths and ideas to improve, while we didn't even mention my hard, time-consuming work keeping to project time schedules. With knowledge of my blind spots I focused more on the joyful part of my job to inspire my teams and put less emphasis on perfect timekeeping.

---

9   M Goldsmith, 'Feed Forward' (Marshall Goldsmith, 2007), https://marshallgoldsmith.com/articles/feed-forward, accessed 7 August 2023

By actively seeking feedforward from those around you, you can identify areas where you can add more value or act differently to improve the outcomes. In this chapter, we'll delve into the benefits of feedforward and I'll offer guidance on implementing it effectively in your organisation. We'll explore different types of feedforward that you can adapt and use to engage your teams even more.

This chapter's rhythm practice is a little different. Here, you'll choose from previous practices that you feel didn't work so well and improve them by asking for feedforward from colleagues. By doing this, you can observe the improvements and take joy and inspiration from seeing what you can gain from incorporating feedforward into your approach.

Let me share with you a story that beautifully demonstrates how feedforward can help us all improve. In kindergarten, a little boy painted a butterfly that didn't look like a live butterfly initially. By asking for open, honest observations for concrete improvement from his classmates and incorporating them into the painting, he created a beautiful picture of a butterfly that everyone admired. In the same way, leaders can improve their business quickly with feedforward from colleagues.

We draw inspiration from playing sports, such as football and basketball, and music, with bands, choirs and orchestras. In both these activities, constant improvement is the norm. It's the same in business. At times, it's essential to pause, relax and take a development holiday to recharge, but ultimately, we need to stretch ourselves, step outside our comfort zones, and try new things to become high-performing, empowered and creative teams.

I hope you find value in the ideas presented in this chapter and wish you fun and success in implementing them. Your teams will appreciate your courage and openness to seeking improvement.

FEEDFORWARD RHYTHM PRACTICE

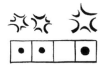 You might have struggled with some of the rhythm exercises from our previous chapters. Don't let this stop you from playing and practising because this exercise is all about embracing and learning from failures.

Choose one of the most challenging rhythm practices you would like to revise. What was good or excellent and what can be improved? Gather feedforward from your colleagues or from listening back over your rhythm practices if you recorded them.

Now retry this practice on your own, paying attention to the received and observed improvement potential. Concentrate on the feedforward you've accumulated and become better prepared. When you feel ready, it's time to practise with the team. You can then enter another round of feedforward to further enhance the synchronised team rhythm and appreciate and applaud your joint achievements.

Exploring opening up with feedforward

This is my favourite part of looking at the transformation of a team, especially if they believe at the start of the journey that they are close to being perfect already. What happens to groups and companies that don't pay attention to developing their skills?

Staying as we are without feedforward

Some team members remain stuck in a blaming mode, believing that if only the others would change, everything would become effective and well run. Some focus on details and count peanuts, forgetting the overall picture and what they could contribute with slight adaptations. Some slow things down with bureaucracy. They are convinced they are always right, which can manifest as a tendency to want control and power over others.

Some tend to speak polemically or even sarcastically. Sarcasm might add unique humour in TV shows and satirical articles, but in a business environment, this kind of criticism belongs to the 'Four Horsemen', Gottman Institute Relationship blog editor Ellie Lisitsa's apocalyptic metaphor for toxic team communications.[10] You will get clarity on the effect this 'Horseman' has on your business organisation by asking your colleagues how they perceive the use of this toxic type of communication in your teams.

Your audience in an environment where these behaviours are rife can often perceive communication as somebody speaking from a self-imagined pedestal. It seems annoying, ridiculous, frustrating and ineffective to colleagues, especially those who have worked in empowered high-performing teams. The result is your best talents will look for another job far away from these toxic behaviours.

This is what happens if we never take any feedforward to adapt to change or try out different actions and behaviours to optimise our teams' potential. On the other hand, what can happen if we challenge our ego from our current reality, looking towards optimal future scenarios?

 Ask yourself, 'What do I need to learn to adapt to change now to best contribute to my team's future?' This question is essential to an open, growth-orientated mindset that values continuous development and embracing new challenges. In the second cartoon, we observe a team whose members practise trust and courage to learn from others. For them, daily feedforward is natural, just like exercising and assessing recordings of previous performances is natural for developing skills further in sports or music.

---

10 E Lisitsa, 'The Four Horsemen: Criticism, contempt, defensiveness, and stonewalling' (The Gottman Institute, no date), https://www.gottman.com/blog/the-four-horsemen-recognizing-criticism-contempt-defensiveness-and-stonewalling/, accessed 7 August 2023

 The teams in the cartoon below proactively seek feedforward to detect and reflect on improvement options, asking:

- How can I act more effectively and innovatively in the future?

- What is worth completely changing or strengthening to add value for our company, shareholders and customers?

Opening up and gaining from feedforward

What happens when our cartoon team regularly asks for feedforward? Regular feedforward strengthens a failure culture, so each individual is encouraged and capable of prototyping and adding more value with concrete actions based on colleagues' responses.

Realising change doesn't have to be complicated. Instead of not responding to your team's requests and creating delays, you can commit to prioritising requests and responding to the most important within one day. Trying to answer every request may be overwhelming and ineffective, so it's better to focus on the top three priorities that add the most value and are realistically achievable.

Similarly, you can commit to smiling at your team members at least twice daily to lighten the mood instead of being too serious. Instead of getting stuck in repetitive discussions, think about your intention before speaking and communicate more effectively. Rather than blaming others, talk about what you want to achieve and ask for help and ideas from your colleagues on how to get there.

Finally, you can gain valuable insights by talking to others about their innovative and diverse perspectives, which helps you think outside the box and come up with new ideas. You can improve your work and personal life by making small but impactful changes like these.

Observe both cartoons and reflect on where you see yourself and your team members currently acting. What is your best way forward, using what you have learned from this section?

SHARING EXPERIENCES FROM DIAGNOSTIC TOOLS

If you want your team to be more like the one in the second cartoon, here are some different options I recommend. Some are simple feedforward questions for a face-to-face reflection with your colleagues and business partners, customers, stakeholders and shareholders, and even friends and family. An effective way to get improvement ideas is to conduct a two-minute feedforward survey among your key contacts, asking just a few questions:

- What is the key benefit from your perspective that I add as a leader for you and our company?

- How can I act more effectively in the future?

- What is worth changing or strengthening to add more value for our company, shareholders and customers?

With the first question, the responses you receive act as inspiration for challenging business days as they reflect what your colleagues, leaders and business partners see and value you for. The responses to the second and third questions, which you may recognise as those asked in the previous section by the team that is opening up and benefiting from feedforward, will give you ideas for concrete improvement actions your environment will recognise. They help you overcome your blind spots and grow skills, with benefits for your teams and company.

Reviewing commitments and celebrating the benefits you and your team have achieved after about six months is a good idea. To keep progressing, conduct a follow-up survey in addition to the responses, data and figures from the scaling statements below. Scaling up commitments based on the first six-month exploration period will allow for continuous progress over time.

Ask your team members to consider these statements:

- I act effectively.

- I ask for other perspectives and options and listen openly before deciding.

- I appreciate my colleagues' ideas even if I
  have a different view.

- I express my ideas clearly.

- I support my colleagues with active and powerful questions
  to find solutions by themselves.

- I act on topics proactively according to our
  customer priorities and shareholder value, aligned with our
  strategies.

The response options are completely agree, agree, neutral,
disagree, completely disagree.

Adding these responses to your survey will provide you with
a guide to setting improvement goals next to the individual
responses. You are likely to be amazed when running your
second round of feedforward after taking concrete action and
exploring how the responses reflect your team's growth in
their contribution.

A collection of inspiring and appreciative responses from your
colleagues acknowledging the value you bring will serve as a
reminder of your positive impact, regardless of any obstacles
that may come your way. You might already have surveys
running and available for you and your team in your
organisation, including comparison figures in your market.

 The key enabler is to look at the responses
with the mindset of what can I take out
of them. How will I act differently based
on them in the future? If you're constantly
defending why the figures are as they are or doubting the
sense of surveys, it wastes your time, depletes your energy
and leaves you feeling low or even in a toxic fight-flight-
freeze mode.

If you want to explore more, I recommend Leadership Excellence for leadership styles and team climate transparency where you see your perception of potential growth.[11] You can compare your figures with how they look from the team's perspective. The diagnostic reports also include beneficial hints and concrete recommendations to improve.

 To continuously enhance essential skills for your team, the speediest two-minute feedforward survey questions are:

- What are key success stories worth sharing with this team?

- How do you rate the effectiveness and positivity/fun of the team on a scale of 1 (low) to 10 (high)?

- What needs to change to get the figure towards 10?

- For a team deep dive, I recommend Team Coaching International diagnostics, found in co-founder Philip Sandahl's book *Teams Unleashed*.[12] This divides your team's work into four quarters:

  1. High positivity–low productivity where everyone is happy with a 'let's have a party' atmosphere, so they're lacking the time investment to co-create business results.

  2. Low productivity–low positivity, with missing business engagement and a toxic environment.

  3. High productivity–low positivity, where teams are focusing on achieving targets and missing appreciation, which can hurt creativity.

---

11   C Tanzer, J Vogt and J Mildner, *Lead Now! Lead effectively in the 21st century* (Books on Demand, 2022)

12   P Sandahl and A Phillips, *Teams Unleashed: How to release the power and human potential of work teams* (Nicholas Brealey Publishing, 2019)

4. High positivity–high productivity, with an inspired and engaged atmosphere and excellent outcomes achieved.

The goal is to move your team towards high positivity–high productivity, where colleagues are having fun, being effective and coming up with innovative ideas. Nobody is perfect, but striving forhigh positivity–high productivity will make a big difference in your team's success.

Working with the Gallup StrengthsFinder helps you to see individual strengths and how to engage with your colleagues emphatically.[13] A person with one of the Top 5 Gallup strengths for details can contribute to planning activities or quality architecture when bits and pieces are required.

When teams come together, they can easily detach from listening to detailed planning or stories. To use this time more effectively and engagingly, ask your audience what they are most interested in and start from one picture to get aligned. The visibility of individuals' and teams' Top 5 Gallup strengths grows understanding and support to gain the most from everyone's strengths and use them wisely depending on the environment.

There are various other team and leadership diagnostics available in the market, but the most critical takeaway is the ability and willingness to gain valuable concrete feedforward. A beneficial transformation will commence with your openness and courage to rise towards more fun in your team and develop the added value you contribute in the future.

---

13   T Rath, *StrengthsFinder 2.0* (Gallup Press, 2007)

Key insights and way forward

Key insights:

- Gain from feedforward surveys, choosing the best-fit option for you and your teams.

- Take ideas and actions for concrete improvement from typical feedforward responses to empower your team.

- Revisit the previous rhythm exercises and see how inviting feedforward helps to get you and your team better synchronised.

Way forward:

- Use your best-match feedforward survey to continuously improve and raise effectiveness.

- Listening to the song 'Not Perfect' by Tim Minchin, as suggested in Chapter 6, helps you to avoid a cut in the connection when you're challenging and stretching your teams, and wanting to be perfect is blocking you from empowering and inspiring them.

9

Awareness For Virtual And Hybrid Teams

This chapter is about different team setups in your business. A combination of team members working from home and spread over various regional offices and across countries.

Generally, virtual and working-from-home office scenarios have increased compared to previous decades, although some leaders still lack trust and want to see their teams working hard with their own eyes. Luckily, this mindset has shifted with the increased agility of technology, and with leaders experiencing during the Covid pandemic the beneficial outcomes resulting from their teams working from home. Leaders then got the opportunity to grow their ability to trust their teams.

We start this chapter by exploring a fun rhythm exercise to help you synchronise virtual or hybrid settings better. Your creative and innovative input will help to get your teams more synchronised.

All leaders are facing similar challenges, so explore what works best for your environment and share great insights with feedforward during your intensive working-from-home times. Some remote colleagues prefer to run informal non-business-related virtual coffee breaks in the morning to keep in touch and strengthen the feeling of team identity. Agile teams could improve their connection by continuing remotely with daily stand-ups (short get-togethers to discuss progress and issues), retrospectives (reflecting on previous scenarios to improve those in the future – similar to feedforward) and demos (to assess the current state of a project). Having a guiding framework promotes a sense of safety, and belonging to a more significant cause than the ego can be especially beneficial when teams are working remotely during challenging times like the pandemic.

Overall, with home working, leaders observed a rise in efficiency with the saving in travelling time, although some leaders and teams mentioned missing the face-to-face exchange in the office space and the fresh air while walking or cycling to and from work. A walk around your neighbourhood can easily replace the journey to the office, although chatting with colleagues from other departments and getting inspired by their different points of view is not easy to replace in virtual setups.

To ensure everyone feels included, we as leaders need to be aware of our colleagues calling in while travelling or joining a meeting virtually. It's vital to ensure that everyone has equal speaking and listening time, regardless of whether they're in the room or attending remotely. Moderation best practices include checking technical setups like echo cancellation and cameras, sharing what's happening in the room, creating exercises that involve everyone, ensuring everyone can contribute to the best possible outcome, avoiding leaving anyone behind and promoting an environment where everyone can participate equally.

What makes a virtual environment different to a physical one? What is the best way to get everyone synchronised? Instead of wanting to go back to the 'good old days', we focus on exploring what is possible, what helps and what supports our new business environment, even if we do not sit with our colleagues in one office space anymore. We can get inspired by the cartoon showing the shift from 'ego' to 'we' and by focusing on contributing to empowering our teams.

Nowadays, many companies give employees space to work from anywhere whenever they want, with the condition that the resultant outcome fits the company's needs. Particularly among the younger generations, people enjoy having the freedom to choose from different options. Some of them love to see each other and spend time together, while others want to choose where to live and work.

In this chapter, I will share observations, best practices and ideas to get the optimal rhythm from your virtual teams. I wish you fun and new insights from these exercises.

VIRTUAL TEAM RHYTHM PRACTICE

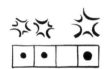 With virtual teams, you often have limited possibilities for communication. These limitations can spark your creativity.

This exercise focuses on speechless communication. Try as a team to play the rhythm together without counting in. You could use eye contact instead. It will probably take a few goes to get it right. Focus on what helps you to synchronise as a virtual team and how you can transport that into your daily work.

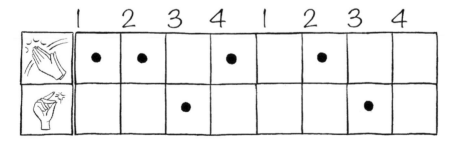

Easy virtual team rhythm practice

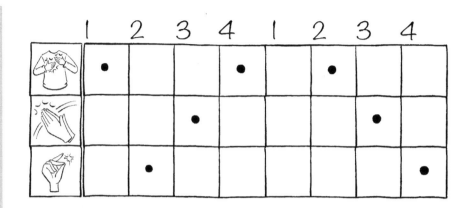

Advanced virtual team rhythm practice

Exploring moving from ego to we for virtual teams

Please feel free to come up with your own thoughts while you're looking at the cartoon demonstrating a transformation from 'ego to we' for a virtually connected team – leaders and employees who work from home or different places, and see and hear each other via video and voice communications.

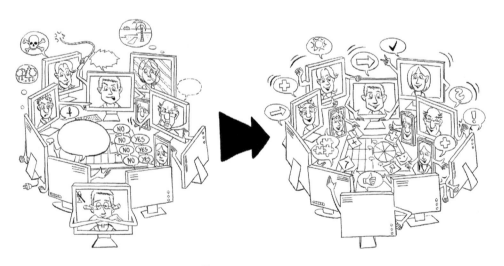

From ego to we

While an ego focus drives the team to have a 'being right' mindset, meaning they're missing solutions and positive outcomes, you can observe in the other half of the cartoon that the 'we' team focus results in a lot of ideas, improvements and creativity on the table in the middle. The team members support each other, encouraging and empowering each other, and creating a highly engaged atmosphere.

What can drive teams from an ego focus to an empowering we focus, especially in a setup that's a mixture of virtual home offices, regional offices and central offices? I've noticed some key differences between people who are effective in these scenarios and those who are not. Productive we-focused team members don't try to exert power over their colleagues, defend their ideas to boost their egos or hide behind the roles, job descriptions or responsibilities as defined in a Responsible, Accountable, Consulted, Informed (RACI) Matrix. This interesting article from expert consultant Paula Martin shows us why the RACI model is the enemy of innovation.[14] They also don't use the excuse 'not my job' to avoid responsibility.

In contrast, ineffective ego-focused teams tend to look for someone to blame when something goes wrong instead of focusing on finding a solution. Then, the never-ending ping-pong of discussions or emails continues wasting time and energy, leading customers and shareholders nowhere. Occasionally, this communication becomes polemical or sarcastic, and it always results in a frustrating and disappointing waste of business- and life-time.

When we're aware of these differences, we can work to avoid negative behaviours and focus on being productive and collaborative. By examining feedforward from employee review platforms like Kununu,[15]

14   P Martin, 'Flush Your RACI Charts Down the Toilet' (Matrix Management Institute, 2020),
      www.matrixmanagementinstitute.com/blog/flush-your-raci-charts-down-toilet , accessed
      7 August 2023

15   Kununu, www.kununu.com

we can gain insight into how ego-driven behaviour is still prevalent in our industries. With continuous development, regular feedforward and self-motivation to grow communication and emotional skills alongside the relevant technical skills, we become a solution-orientated, appreciating-other-colleagues'-ideas-and-perspectives team.

AWARENESS FOR VIRTUAL TEAMS EXERCISE

What differs for a virtual home-office team and needs special attention? This exercise raises focus and attentiveness for mixed virtual and office setups.

Name: Awareness for virtual teams.

Benefit: Raises focus and awareness and supports effective communication, ensuring everyone is heard. This exercise sharpens your team members' listening and speaking antennae to hear and understand each other, and helps your future communication.

Number of participants: Five to fifteen.

Space: Any virtual team setup like Zoom, Teams etc.

Length: For Part 1, one to five minutes.

Part 1: Count from one to n, where n = number of team members in your meeting. One team member starts counting, and then the next one continues the count with the next number, so four team members count in a virtual round from one to four, all paying close attention to their colleagues until everyone has added one number. The counting is meant to run fluently without anyone interrupting each other. Whenever you hear more than one person vocalising the same number, restart your count from one.

Length: For Part 2, ten to thirty minutes.

Part 2: Each team member shares one critical achievement since the team last met as an elevator speech. The presentation contains new and creative ideas from the achievement as well as the intended benefits. Each speaker keeps to their allocated time and brings their speech to a natural conclusion to allow for a smooth and easy handover to the next speaker. A high level of attentiveness, observing mimicry and gestures and the ability to step back and support each other with empathy skills and curiosity are required to communicate effectively.

Length: For Part 3, five to ninety minutes, depending on your choice from the option list below.

Part 3: Please choose from these best practices for virtual, office and hybrid teams, and adapt them to your environment:

- Consider establishing a virtual creative coffee or tea break at the same time and with the same colleagues you would take a break with in the physical office space. Take inspiration from them, helping you find solutions or learnings from diverse experiences.

- Choose a moderator, but consider rotating this role to grow moderation skills and ensure every team member is heard with equal and adequate speaking time. The moderator checks the technical setup upfront, explains movements or changes such as a team member leaving the room or a team that has moved closer to the whiteboard and shares anything that has caused laughter, especially for the virtual participants or those calling while travelling. They ensure that all participants are equally included in the discussions and exercises, for example by asking if anyone has a good idea on how to make sure everyone contributes optimally.

- Consider using visual pictures of a solution, clarifying dependencies or future scenarios and benefits and taking care that all intentions are shown and understood.

- Regularly ask for volunteers among the participants to summarise the content of the meeting, making sure everyone is on the same page.

- Pause and review, adding a question to the virtual team call chat, asking, for example, where people see the team's effectiveness on a scale of one to ten, or use Mentimeter,[16] questions on where you are regarding effectiveness, creativity, innovation, assertive communication and solution orientation, followed by an open-ended discussion on concrete improvement actions to scale up whenever appropriate.

- Clarify upfront what you intend to achieve when you've completed this meeting. What are the results you're aiming for in three months? What do you want the participants still to remember in one year?

- Make sure everyone, in the room or attending virtually, agrees to be present and willing to include and hear everyone equally.

16   Mentimeter, www.mentimeter.com

- Complete the meeting with concrete commitments to take action, discussing the value everyone has gained from the meeting and collecting ideas to be even more effective next time.

- You can gain from everyone having as much time as they need to talk about their learnings from a project or co-creation in their team, finishing with one final takeaway sentence.

Even though these exercises and practices are helpful for office teams, they are even more critical for virtual and hybrid teams. I hope you and your organisation will enjoy the added value of the outcomes.

Key insights and way forward

Key insights:

- Improve synchronisation with the help of the rhythm exercise by focusing on eye contact in virtual setups.

- Gain inspiration from best practices for virtual, hybrid and office teams.

- Practise more efficient communication with the counting exercise.

Way forward:

- For meetings and offsites, ensure that all ideas are heard, every expert is included, especially participants calling in while travelling to the meeting or joining virtually, and the technical setup is validated upfront. Consider working with an experienced moderator to support effective communication and improve outcomes.

- Gain from your and your team's creativity to adapt and get an optimal outcome from your meeting or workshop.

- Share your intentions with a visual picture of your aims and what your team is supposed to remember in one year.

- Make it your intention to spend valuable business- and life-time in any of your meetings.

10

Make Full Use Of Diversity

Welcome to the chapter on gaining from diverse teams. In today's world, where globalisation has brought multiple cultures together, it's essential to embrace people's differences and bring them together to create a cohesive team. The purpose of this chapter is to explore the benefits of diversity in teams and how to leverage it to achieve better results.

Everyone has a unique background shaped by their culture, religion, gender, age, sexual orientation, education and life experiences. It's a diversity of backgrounds that creates an opportunity to bring together unique perspectives, which helps drive innovation and creativity. In this chapter, we will explore how you can contribute to your diverse team's success by sharing your values, enthusiasm and wisdom passed on from your parents and grandparents.

Your work experience also plays a significant role in your contribution to the team. If you've worked in different industries and countries, you can provide valuable insights. Whether you are introverted, extroverted, optimistic, humorous or severe, your strengths are valuable and beneficial to drive optimal outcomes.

Research shows that diverse teams can lead to more creative, innovative and customer-focused outcomes.[17, 18] However, in such teams, it's essential to have excellent communication skills to ensure that everyone's voice is heard and opinions are appreciated. In this chapter, we will work together, contributing our unique experiences and strengths towards sustainable, valuable business outcomes.

The rhythm exercise will explore playing innovative and creative beats as a diverse team, paying attention to the beauty of the empty spaces between the beats. Music becomes inspiring when there are pauses in between the tones. You will get new insights by looking at the cartoon scenarios, where a diverse team nearly collapses through a lack of communication skills, while another enjoys high-level empathy conversations, taking and leveraging each other's viewpoints.

With this chapter, I hope to inspire you to embrace diversity and gain from the many benefits it can offer.

DIVERSITY RHYTHM PRACTICE

The rhythm in both teams and music consists of beats and pauses. More often than not, the pauses – what you are not playing or saying – are more important than what you are playing.

Silence creates a free space for a full exchange of ideas, for improvisation. You must have already strengthened your

17 A Jõgi, 'Diverse Teams Achieve Greater Success: How business can champion diversity as good sense' (Forbes, 2022), www.forbes.com/sites/forbestechcouncil/2022/05/10/diverse-teams-achieve-greater-success-how-business-can-champion-diversity-as-good-sense/?sh=2193fe2d560e, accessed 7 August 2023

18 S Dixon-Fyle, K Dolan, V Hunt and S Prince, 'Diversity Wins: How inclusion matters' (McKinsey & Co, 2020), www.mckinsey.com/featured-insights/diversity-and-inclusion/diversity-wins-how-inclusion-matters, accessed 7 August 2023

rhythm practices from Chapter 1, 'Raise Your Listening Skills', and Chapter 6, 'Growing Trust', and enhanced your leadership presence skills from Chapter 3, 'Grow Your Leadership Presence', before attempting this exercise. You'll need to combine all those skills to gain from diverse improvisations.

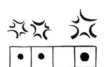 Improvise with a stomp and clap in the easy exercise. With advanced practice, you can choose any accent you prefer. First, you improvise independently and record your most enjoyable rhythm into a copy of the empty notation table shown in the illustrations.

	1	2	3	4	1	2	3	4
👣								
👏								

Easy gaining from diversity rhythm practice

	1	2	3	4	1	2	3	4

Advanced gaining from diversity rhythm practice

Then you present your ideas to the rest of the team and listen attentively to everyone's creative grooves. You complete with an inspiring joint team improvisation, including all the diverse rhythms.

You may want to find your individual start and end rhythm contribution without counting in, as we explored during the rhythm practice in Chapter 9, 'Awareness For Virtual And Hybrid Teams'. You can even consider recording your rhythms or giving a stage performance at the next company celebration event.

Exploring diversities from blaming to gaining

After playing all the tones so far from our xylophone model, you have explored more than enough to empower and inspire your team to move from blaming towards gaining from diversity. In this chapter, all these skills come together so you naturally become curious to learn more about your team's diverse pathways, backgrounds, skills and values.

Let's first take a look at the blaming, ego-focused diverse team. One colleague is an introvert with tremendous expert knowledge. He is convinced nobody is interested in his thoughts and opinions, so he keeps silent. Another expert could provide international best practices from different industries to enhance the team's results, but as she is not a native speaker of the prevailing language, she decides to stay quiet so as not to risk being blamed if things go wrong or laughed at. One person is shouting at a wall. He believes he is the only clever person in the room and wants to convince the team, but his loud, misleading assumptions have caused everyone else to turn their back towards him.

Two people who have been through organisational restructures and redundancies in the past express themselves using sarcasm, irony and polemic, gossiping about others. They have sneers on their faces and a finger is pointing at the leader who is just entering the room. A more senior member of the team sits with his mug of tea, dreaming of the past and wondering where it all went wrong, keeping his decades of relevant experience to himself. This team looks more like a nightmare than a group of professional businesspeople.

Diversities from blaming to gaining – the blaming team

In the gaining cartoon, we notice a team curious to learn from each other. They regularly exercise synchronisation skills of active listening and improving their presence. They raise their effectiveness by using feedforward to develop their skills continuously. Crucially, they show a high level of trust in each other.

This team comes together with a shared picture of a successful optimal outcome for their meeting. They are keen to find out more about each other's different skills, perspectives and knowledge. They want to discover how existing diversities can add tremendously to a valuable outcome. Everyone in the group feels appreciated, trusting that their values are respected and accepted. This atmosphere leads to open and creative communication and fruitful discussions.

Diversities from blaming to gaining – the gaining team

The introvert draws a picture, including different options and a transparent view of all related dependencies. The team is glad to have such a skilful expert who can simplify complex scenarios into one understandable drawing. The colleague with international multi-industry best practices knowledge shares one of her solutions that worked successfully in a similar environment. Notice her inspired facial expression as she talks to her colleague who, in the first cartoon, was the man shouting at the wall. He is now actively listening and interested in his colleague's diverse expertise.

The two cynics have changed their communication style from sarcasm and polemic and are looking enthusiastically at the simple clarifying picture on the whiteboard. One of them adds an idea of how to streamline. His colleague nods appreciatively and draws a smiley face next to the drawing. The senior staff member, with all his knowledge about the impact of reorganisation and change on teams, contributes with a new idea about a best-fit structure arrangement for the meeting outcome.

Let's leave them to continue gaining from their diversities and exploring them more and more to lead towards an optimal outcome. We will now move forward to look at a manifesto for a diverse team and how this can support your organisation.

TEAM ALIGNMENT AND HOW BEST TO ACHIEVE IT

How do you take advantage of a team manifesto or alignment, especially for a diverse team? Looking at the manifesto of agile values and principles and adapting it for teams outside of software development is one best practice. Here's an example of what I mean, paraphrased from the original:[19]

We value **individuals and interactions** more than processes and tools, and **customer and user benefits** more than detailed documentation, **and responding to change** more than following a plan.

Even though there is value in all the practices noted in this manifesto, you value the ones in bold type more. You follow the principles:

---

19   Manifesto for Agile Software Development, https://agilemanifesto.org

- The highest priority is to satisfy the external customer and end users of our product or service through early and continuous delivery of valuable results.

- The team welcomes changes even late in the project.

- The team focuses on adding value for customers and users in regular demos. All interested leaders are welcome.

- Involved leaders provide the team members with a safe environment to innovate, support their needs and trust them to realise their committed actions.

- The team members communicate regularly in an effective exchange and support each other in finding solutions for upcoming obstacles.

- The team members communicate proactively and respectfully, being solution-orientated and focusing on demo targets.

- The team members are open to continuous development of their communication skills and adapt their behaviour to achieve added value.

- Simplification is essential. The team avoids activities not necessary for the outcome.

- Colleagues regularly reflect on effectiveness, positivity and innovation to grow continuously towards becoming an empowered high-performing team.

You can craft a team manifesto that aligns with your values and views by engaging in the empowering team exercise coming up. The resulting agreement will create a safe and secure space where team members can openly share their thoughts and contribute ideas. Ultimately, this will lead to a more trusting and co-creating business environment.

Name: Creating your best-fit team manifesto.

Benefit: A safe, inspirational space to strengthen gaining from diversities.

Number of participants: Five to twelve.

Space: A virtual or office room.

Length: Sixty minutes.

1. Start with a five-minute time investment to think about the best-ever team practices from your background experience. Share specific behaviour that led to the most beneficial highlights.

2. Divide the team into three to five sub-teams, identifying specific values and best communication practices you want to establish and strengthen in your sub-team.

3. Once you've identified these practices, you can work on defining what they mean specifically for your sub-team. Disruptive questions can be helpful here, such as 'What does this phrase mean exactly?' or 'How will this add value to our future team co-creation?' By asking these questions, you can dive deeper into each practice and ensure that you clearly understand what it entails.

Another critical aspect of effective teamwork is identifying communication behaviours and patterns that are unacceptable to the team. These can include things like interrupting or blaming others and lacking attentiveness. You need to work on developing strategies for addressing these behaviours and patterns when they arise. To do this, you identify the underlying causes of the behaviours and address them proactively. One part of the sub-team works on identifying beneficial and effective ways to handle conflicts and escalation, ensuring that the resolution is fair, respectful and solution-orientated. The other identifies ways to align decision-making and drive decisions to become realised.

Finally, you work on identifying communication practices that support simplification and solution orientation. Still in sub-teams, you pinpoint the practices supporting team identity and co-creation.

4. Each sub-team presents their outcomes. Everyone else in the group provides feedforward to refine and improve the outcomes until there is consensus about team alignment.

5. Everyone shares from their point of view and background the benefits and values they appreciate most from the co-created team manifesto. They then all commit to following the agreed alignment for a prototype period.

I recommend that you continuously improve the team co-creation manifesto agreement beyond the prototype period.

BEST COMMUNICATION PRACTICES WHEN CORE-VALUE BOUNDARIES ARE CROSSED

I'd like to share an exercise that helps to create a respectful and safe environment for a diverse team. Curiosity will allow you to have fun and lively experiences with your team while doing this exercise.

Name: Visualise core-value diversity boundaries.

Benefit: Awareness and respect for individual boundaries in the team help to raise trust and provide a safe space for everyone to speak up freely and gain from diversities.

Number of participants: Five to twelve.

Space: In an office or virtual setup with a whiteboard to visualise your team members' boundaries.

Length: Forty to sixty minutes.

1. Exchange one of your diverse contribution stories. What story do you typically like to share with your colleagues so they understand your core values better? It could be anything you remember fighting for as you couldn't ignore your inner voice or something special you'd like your colleagues to know about you.

2. Draw a wall on the whiteboard. Place yourself individually in front of this wall.

3. Visualise with drawings or write what is crucial for you. This stays on the other side of the wall.

4. Share your visualisation with your colleagues, explaining the behaviours you consider inappropriate or off-limits because they violate your core values.

5. When everyone has completed steps 1–4, commit as a team to appreciating and respecting each other's boundaries, and establish an agreement for handling situations where people unintentionally cross them. Remember, nobody is perfect, and cultivating a culture of learning from failure is motivating and beneficial in the long run.

Alternatively, you can use communication best practices for any challenging situation. Whenever someone crosses your core value, cultural or ethical boundary while communicating with you before you have an agreement for handling this situation in place, choose the response that fits best for you and adapt the wording to your authentic way of speaking:

- We are all here to achieve our company targets and to add our expertise in a solution-orientated way. What exactly is the aim of this statement?

- What is your intention? What concrete result do you want to achieve with your message?

- I want to clarify the impact of this communication. My core ethical values boundary has been crossed here and I feel (for example) embarrassed/hurt/intimidated. How can we communicate effectively next time in a similar situation without crossing any value boundaries so that we can focus on our target achievements and accept our diverse perspectives and expertise?

- Freedom of speech ends for one of us when the dignity and values of the other are at risk of being violated. Do you agree?

- We take care of our ethical company cultural values, which align with the United Nations' goals and human rights. Our communication is supposed to strengthen our team identity so we all gain from our individual and team strengths in a way that makes sure each of us feels safe and appreciated. Do you agree?

- What is your intention in using that expression here? How about we look at your suggestion from a joint solution- and success-orientated perspective?

- How can we better communicate in future, ensuring a solution focus to effectively avoid crossing each other's or our company's value boundaries? What words, mimicry and gestures cause our cultural boundaries to be crossed and hurt our dignity? How can we avoid this and instead speak and act in a solution-focused and appreciative manner?

Prepare yourself well for this clarifying one-to-one conversation with your colleague (eg take a deep breath and avoid rushing your words, be aware of the optimal outcome of the clarification exchange and share your agreements at the end of the one-to-one time). These best practices are intended to help you become even stronger through the challenge of communication in a diverse team, so both parties gain new insights and learnings from your exchange.

Key insights and way forward

Key insights:

- Explore enablers to move from blaming to gaining from diversities in your team.

- Clarity about what you can take from the Agile Software Development Manifesto to establish a safe space to gain the most from your diverse teams.

- Raise awareness and respect for individual boundaries in the team.

- Rhythm consists of pauses and tones. Silence as well as the sound of voices lead to a co-creating team communication. Examine the beneficial effects on innovation of joint moments of silence in the rhythm exercise.

Way forward:

- Clarify boundaries using visualisation and co-create a team manifesto aligned with any new diverse team setup. Continuously refresh your boundaries visualisation and team alignment, being curious about natural changes.

- Celebrate the achievements of your diverse team and the contributions of each person from various perspectives, experiences and core values.

- Continue to have fun and gain new insights with the improvisation rhythm exercise.

11

Gaining From Areas Outside Your Business

As a leader, you bring your unique experiences and perspectives from various areas of your life into your daily actions. Have you ever noticed that these experiences can also empower your team? By sharing your passions outside of work, such as sports, music, sailing, meditation or volunteering, with your team members, and encouraging them to share theirs, you can tap into a wealth of skills and knowledge to help you become an even more effective leader.

In this chapter, I would love to share my experience of stepping out of my business focus to explore four different areas: jazz bands, sports exercises, film production and agile software development. We will then conclude with a celebration team rhythm exercise.

What can we learn to help diverse teams come together by looking at jazz bands? Taking advantage of established structures ensures everyone in the band gets a chance to improvise and shine in the spotlight. Whenever band members pay attention to the other musicians around them, the sound they make grooves.

I'm delighted in this chapter to share an insight from an incredible motivational sports coach, Linda Zanin, who has contributed one of her engaging boot camp exercises for you. Also from the world of sport, the health and mobility exercise will challenge your team members' brains while helping to keep you all fit. You can explore this as a short intervention in the office, during an offsite event or even remotely.

Joining various film productions during my years spent living near Munich, I was impressed by observing so many people coming together in what appeared to be a chaotic manner. To begin with, I couldn't see any structural approach and wondered how the chaos could ever become a coherent filmed scene at the end of the day. In fact, I spent most of my time asking myself, 'What the hell are all these people doing?' However, by the end of my first film production experience, I'd figured out how each person added their expertise to the scene by focusing on the moment of silence before the filming started. This is similar to business production, where all is timed precisely to the point where the product goes live and all the parts come together.

When we look at agile software development teams, what can we learn from them? It is worth examining their failure culture, trust and approach. Agile team members count on one another to gain clarity on the added value for the end users and customers, and welcome changes along the way.

The structure of this chapter differs a little from the others. The rhythm exercise comes at the end, as it focuses on concluding your journey to *Team Rhythm* with a celebration, having fun and coming together.

Exploring what we can learn from bands to gain from diversity

I want to share with you my jazz band experience, looking at improving the sound through the use of a clearly communicated structure and intention.

An essential part of the development of a song consists of an agreement between the musicians on a reproducible form – a separation into verses, refrain and bridge. On the one hand, the structure covers the song as a whole, the order in which each band member will play, who will play when over how many pulses and which parts need to be aligned. On the other hand, it includes decisions about the solo arrangement, alternating the melody instruments with the drums or using a combination of instruments in turn during one solo. This clear, complete framework provides the basis for fluent and free improvisation. The more synchronised the rhythm instruments are, the easier improvisation is for the melody instruments and the more the musicians' enthusiasm can come across to the audience.

A synchronised rhythm, listening skills and full attention from the band when the soloists are performing all play an essential role in the brilliance of improvisation in music. The soloist profits from this, along with their experience with their instrument, to deliver a clear intention and message for the audience.

Each soloist's development practice consists of staying focused, being present with their body and mind and being fully engaged. One useful exercise for band members' preparation consists of listening to and analysing recordings of their performances, especially if they get the opportunity to gain feedforward from their audience. Another continuous learning exercise that significantly affects audience enjoyment is a band member observing other musicians, looking for attractive concrete styles and methods and deciding which are worth including in their solos, which fit their authentic style.

What can you take from these band exercises and incorporate as a leader in your daily business routines for your teams and organisation?

USING EXERCISE TO ENHANCE TEAM ENGAGEMENT FOR REGULAR MEETINGS AND OFFSITES

Please take a moment to think. How long have you been sitting at your computer or in meetings today? When was the last time you stood up? If it's been over half an hour, please stand up right now and complete this short exercise.

Name: Health and mobility check.

Benefit: Raised awareness and motivation, enhancing your health and mobility.

Number of participants: One.

Space: Wherever you are.

Length: One minute.

1. Stand upright with your feet together.

2. Bend forward and see how far you can reach with your fingertips towards your feet or the floor. It's important to keep your knees straight the whole time.

If you have a healthy level of mobility, you should be able to touch the floor with your fingertips. Can't do it? Then you're definitely sitting too much.

Studies from the United States have confirmed that to counteract the negative impacts on our health of sitting for too long, we should take a five-minute walk for every thirty minutes we spend sitting.[20] Walking positively affects mobility, lowers blood pressure and improves blood sugar levels.

I wish you great fun with this next exercise from Linda Zanin,[21] which will help with successful meetings:

Name: I pack my sports bag.

Benefit: A raised team awareness and a lightened-up atmosphere while strengthening your fitness.

Number of participants: Five to twelve people. If there are more than twelve people in the meeting, form sub-teams of around six people.

Space: You can easily integrate physical activities into offsites or standard Zoom conferences. Office attire is adequate for exploring this practice.

Length: Five to ten minutes.

One person picks a well-known workout exercise and puts it in an imaginary sports bag. The next colleague adds another workout activity to the first one in the bag. The entire team or sub-team jointly practises each selected sports bag exercise, one after another. Each team member takes a turn adding an exercise until everyone has contributed.

20   AT Duran et al, 'Breaking Up Prolonged Sitting to Improve Cardiometabolic Risk: Dose–response analysis of a randomized crossover trial', *Medicine & Science in Sports & Exercise*, 55(5) (1 May 2023) 847–855

21   Linda Zanin via www.instagram.com/fitmit.linda/ or fitmitlinda.personaltraining@gmail.com

Do some exercise

You can choose from workout exercises such as squats, arm circles, jumping on the spot, lunges, nodding, knee raises, clapping, hip circles, standing on one leg and circling feet, or creating your own innovative practices. It is helpful to nominate one team member to record and monitor every exercise going into the sports bag so they are performed in the correct order.

For example:

Person 1: I pack my sports bag and put in:

- Five arm circles backwards (everyone circles their arms)

Person 2: I pack my sports bag and put in:

- Five arm circles backwards (everyone circles their arms)
- Five jumping on the spot (everyone jumps on the spot)

Person 3: I pack my sports bag and put in:

- Five arm circles backwards (everyone circles their arms)

- Five jumping on the spot (everyone jumps on the spot)

- Five nods (everyone nods)

When a team member can no longer pack all the exercises in the correct order into the sports bag, you pause the game and the person can choose to start over or restart with the first exercise from the beginning of the practice. You complete the game when everyone has successfully packed their exercise into the sports bag.

You can choose to repeat this exercise between three and ten times to raise the brain's attention. A mix of number of repetitions during the exercise can make it even more challenging and fun.

This game provides variety and movement, trains attention, memory and creativity and is suitable for all fitness levels. Most importantly, it's fun. Even the most accomplished and well-known athletes like to do something new or challenging that takes them outside of what they are used to or comfortable with, so give it a try and get started.

Exploring what we can gain from film production

Welcome to immersing yourself in film production for leadership inspiration. For the next few minutes, viewing the world through the eyes of a film crew will guide you to new opening-up questions and actions for your future team successes.

For film productions, word beats like 'Sound action', 'Sound is running', 'Quiet, please', 'Focus' and 'Action' help actors find the attention they need for a successful film scene outcome. You can feel a muscular tension arising from the intense moments of silence just before the first scene claps. The focus is on the relationship between the actors. Their body language, impressions and movements express emotions.

Scenes are developed by beats of spoken words with various tones and pitches of voice. Sound volumes and rhythms capture and win over the audience. Those beats trigger changes for scene optimisation until the result is acknowledged by applause from the whole film crew.

The best positioning and development of numerous existing film roles are decided based on planning ideas from the stage director. Which actor fits which role? Which behaviour from individual characters can be developed outside of the action? What influence can a strong actor bring into their role play?

Exploration and optimisation during the scenes belong naturally to the progression of film productions. Every leading and supporting actor has their own contribution and spotlight. The camera team looks carefully at all details before and during the shoot for optimal light and shadow conditions. Whenever distracting shadows appear, the director's attention shifts from the actors towards the camera team. Costume and makeup experts stay near the set, present and ready to jump in for alterations during breaks between the scenes.

The extras provide background movement, advised by the stage director's assistant, to enhance the atmosphere. Their performance is triggered by word beats from the leading actors during the scene play, which give the whole film crew orientation. The last part of the production is done without the camera, when the sound engineers put the microphone into the vital centre spot, with the final recording of sound effects to complete the filming.

What we can learn from film production

Synchronous alignments for the scenes are driven mainly by the stage
director's assistant, who ensures that all sub-team arrangements are
guided effectively to the first beat of the first scene. This means the stage
director can focus on the big picture: the film outcome and its effect
on the audience. Each sub-team – sound, camera, makeup, costume,
catering, production, actors and extras – contributes with asynchronous
foundation beats and individual preparations towards the start of the film
scene.

Camera and sound assistants ensure optimal lighting and the best sound.
They plan scenes while remaining highly sensitive to all related details.
Costume and makeup artists are thinking about the best fit concerning
makeup and clothing for the actors and extras in the film. Days before the
filming, each extra receives a briefing describing what they are required
to wear. They then choose a variety of costumes that fit their role and the
film's location.

One key message to the crew to ensure focus and attention is 'Quiet, please – we are filming'. Sources of interference are swiftly found and addressed. For some film productions, a unique role exists to protect the film crew and scene from outside disturbances.

 What concrete lessons can you take from film shoots to drive your project success? When you step from the office building into the outside world after completing the tasks – filming the last scene – of your day, take your time to reflect. How did today's sets look? Which words and sentences led to a positive movement and change? Which words strengthened a transparent and clear focus? Which raised emotions? How did your team handle those emotions?

What do the responses to these questions mean for your business's success and added value? Who on the team took care of effective synchronisation and aligned co-creation? Who ensured honest, transparent and solution-orientated communication? Did you give acknowledgement and appreciation after an inspiring team success? Did you recognise moments full of attention? Who protected your team from turbulence from the outside and ensured the required focus for valuable outcomes?

What would your business production film look like? How will you prepare yourself for tomorrow's planned scenes? How is your production team doing? What shift of attention will your team need tomorrow? How can you act to empower your team even more? What is your conclusion from your observations and thoughts on today's business scenes from a film production perspective?

Exploring what we can use from agile software development teams

We talked in the previous chapter about the Agile Manifesto,[22] but the wording is specific to software development. However, we can apply the agile pull approach to other business teams to increase engagement. This means that whenever a team member completes a task, they then pull the next one, according to their skills and the order of priority, from the team's to-do list. Instead of giving commands, we can inspire and define the goals of the organisation and clarify what exactly leads to excellence for the end users and customers.

It's important to remember that agile is not a one-size-fits-all approach. Some colleagues may prefer to be given clear commands and specific tasks to complete. Others may enjoy having more creative freedom and working collaboratively with their team to achieve well-defined targets.

One positive aspect of an agile team is its members' autonomy to make decisions. They share responsibility and do not waste time defining roles. Instead, they clarify goals and create value for their product or service's customers or users. They commit to their goals and pull activities aligned with their strengths and expertise towards their desired outcomes instead of pushing each other to take action. They look at how they can support each other, regularly examining achievements and finding solutions for blockers. These teams continuously reflect to develop and grow their abilities to become more and more realistic about what they can achieve.

---

22   Manifesto for Agile Software Development, https://agilemanifesto.org

Instead of complaining and going into a fight-flight-freeze mode when unexpected obstacles or issues show up during a project, agile teams welcome change even late in the development phase. Their focus is on clarifying why they have decided to make a change. Why now? They maintain transparency when they determine the changes that will add customer or shareholder value or support them with their strategies. Hence, the changes are visible to everyone impacted.

Pairing is worth exploring for your business as four eyes see more than two, especially when you're looking from a quality perspective and want to gain from diverse expertise for your market's services or products. Presenting achievements in standard timeframes, for example, a twenty minute presentation every two weeks, to users or customers raises team identity, which helps people to adapt to a well-matched team rhythm.

Looking at the other side, teams with project managers tend to be controlled by a traffic light system. A change from a green to a red light when an issue occurs shortly before a deadline leads to everyone downing tools and looking for the guilty party. What's the point of keeping this system running? Instead of playing the blame game, which has the effect that nobody dares to be honest about their mistakes, grow from your everyday experiences and identify options.

 What would a solution look like? What ideas do you have as a team? What are you going to do differently next time, learning from this failure? What will help you to grow your failure culture and establish an entirely engaging team atmosphere?

COMPLETION CELEBRATION RHYTHM

What can we learn from music? From bands and rhythm in general? Now that you've gained expertise in the world of rhythm, what is your takeaway?

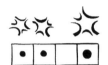 As a celebration of the completion of your journey to *Team Rhythm*, tap and clap together as a team to a well-known song. You can choose from two easy and two advanced song ideas for your final rhythm exercise. Get on stage and have fun!

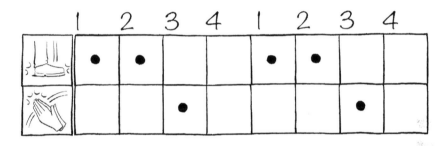

Easy celebration rhythm: 'We Will Rock You' – Queen

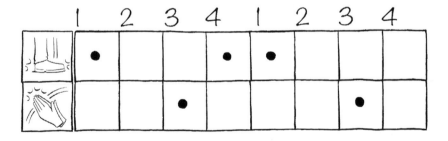

Easy celebration rhythm: 'Every Breath You Take' – The Police

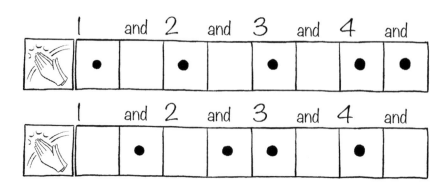

Advanced celebration rhythm: 'Viva La Vida' – Coldplay

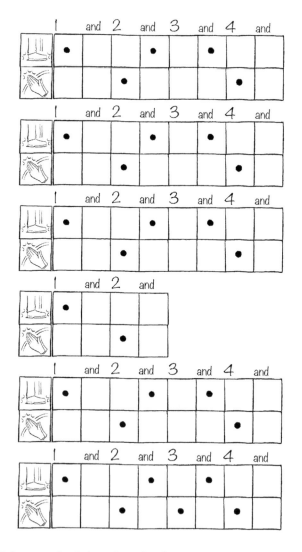

Advanced celebration rhythm: 'Hey Ya!' – Outkast

Another even more creative option is to choose the rhythm from your favourite song or compose a new rhythm song. This will help raise your team's identity and connection and appreciation of each other, concluding with a tremendous round of applause.

Key insights and way forward

Key insights:

- Raise your team's atmosphere by looking at a jazz band's rehearsals and learning how their structure and direction can help.

- Gain new ideas from film productions and how working in one direction helps teams to get aligned.

- Enlighten your team and strengthen mobility with the sports bag packing exercise.

- Raise creativity and motivation in your business by looking at what works well for agile software development teams and how it can work for you.

Way forward:

- Explore the exercises with your teams while enjoying new experiences.

- Invite customers and users of your product or service to your achievement demonstrations.

- Establish and strengthen a learning-from-failure culture.

- Regularly take a break. Step outside of your business environment, look around and take insights from nature to empower and inspire your teams.

- Celebrate successes with your team.

Conclusion

Team Rhythm has taken us on a journey of exploring different exercises and practices to improve team co-creation and efficiency. We have examined raising skills via rhythm practices on each tone of the xylophone model, gained insights from cartoons and learned from areas outside our business environment to inspire and empower our teams to increase business value.

A transformation from feeling overwhelmed to becoming an inspired, high-performing team will not happen overnight. However, there are various way-forward options on your continuous improvement journey. You are welcome to contact me via my webpage, aiccoaching.com, so we can co-create further skill enhancement from the xylophone model. Together, we can focus either on individual tones or on tone combinations, helping you and your team become more synchronised, raising efficiency and empowering your team, leading to an improved valuable outcome.

Another way forward is to take time off to walk along a river, by the sea or in the mountains. Feel the flow next to you, enjoy the impressive mountain view or watch the powerful waves crash on the shore. The majesty of nature helps you maintain your leadership presence. Alternatively, visit inspirational places like art galleries or museums. Even computer-animated visuals can create impressions, providing you with new ideas.

Regularly challenging yourself and your team, ensuring alignment and clarifying that your intentions and strategies are fully understood, helps raise efficiency. Encouraging your team to contribute their ideas and views to the whole picture strengthens connection and speeds up achieving the excellence you seek.

I'm looking forward to hearing your insights and thoughts. I highly appreciate your courage in being open and willing to improve continuously.

I wish you all the best for your team's empowerment and your organisation's great success.

Further Resources

Goldsmith, M, *What Got You Here Won't Get You There: How successful people become even more successful* (Profile Books, 2008)

Gupta, SR, *A Quick Guide to Cultural Competency* (Second Edition, Gupta Consulting Group, 2016)

Johnson, S, *Who Moved My Cheese?: An amazing way to deal with change in your work and in your life* (Vermilion, 2002)

Kniberg, H, 'Agile Everywhere – slides from my keynote at Lean Forum' (Crisp's blog, 2018), https://blog.crisp.se/2018/10/17/henrikkniberg/agile-everywhere-slides-from-my-keynote-at-lean-forum

Kniberg, H, 'Spotify Engineering Culture – Part 2 (aka the "Spotify Model")' (YouTube, 2019), www.youtube.com/watch?v=vOt4BbWLWQw

Sjöstrand, B, *OUTSTANDING in the MIDDLE: How middle managers make the difference* (Panoma Press, 2020)

Tedx Talks, 'Music Paradigm: Roger Nierenberg at TEDxRiversideAvondale' (YouTube, 2013), www.youtube.com/watch?v=QE8Sj_nggp0

Acknowledgements

First, I want to acknowledge and applaud my youngest son David for the idea of including rhythm practices and for each team rhythm skill composition from the xylophone model. Many thanks also to Sophie Hendler for your patience and practice exploration.

I highly appreciate Lukas, my middle son, for his business consulting, look and feel overview and clear pictures, and Magda Jackwerth for adding value with a detailed beta reading from the perspective of young talent in the telecommunication business.

Thank you to Christoph, my eldest son, and Theresa Kranz for the encouragement to write *Team Rhythm*.

Huge applause and appreciation to the professional and creative cartoonist Mele Brink. Cartoons are a real highlight for all of my programmes, and they help to illustrate the scenarios in *Team Magic* and *Team Rhythm*.

I am grateful to Linda Zanin for the addition of one of her engaging sports boot camp exercises.

Thanks to my publisher, Rethink, for the inspirational writing and reviewing journey. Without Lucy McCarraher and Joe Gregory's mentoring to write my manuscript in ninety days, this book would have taken years of writing and maybe never have been completed.

I highly appreciate and thank all my beta readers for their valuable feedforward to improve *Team Rhythm*: Ari Ovaskainen, Harco Smit, Gerald Seggewies, Steve Cockerell, Andrea and Andreas Kranz.

Finally, I sincerely applaud all my clients for their trustful co-creation and willingness to improve and empower their teams.

The Author

During the last thirty-two years, Iris Clermont has been living her passion in twenty different countries worldwide as a combination of a team and leadership coach and business consultant for corporate companies. She shared her experience by writing her first number one bestselling book, *Team Magic: Eleven ways for winning teams*, eleven years ago, and has now followed that up with new insights and advice in *Team Rhythm: Eleven ways to lead your team from overwhelmed to inspired*.

A certified mathematician passionate about empowering leaders and teams, she enhanced her coaching skills with certifications from Team Coaching International and Conversational Intelligence to offer diagnosis reports and tools based on figures and facts. Additionally, she holds a Professional Accreditation from the International Coaching Federation, which upholds a high ethical standard.

Her vision is to make you smile. Her mission is to motivate teams to work effectively and be solution-orientated and creative while having fun and gaining energy from their business life for their private life and vice versa. For her, a programme is only successful when each participant gains real value from the outcomes and can use the new insights in their business and home life. This success is evident in the smiling faces: the contented smiles of leaders and teams who achieve alignment in their personal and business targets. Her best motivation comes from the smiles of teams co-developing effectively, just like the co-creative cartoon scenarios from *Team Rhythm*, with all members looking to add the same value and move in the same direction while appreciating each other, developing skills and contributing to the outcomes.

You can get in touch with Iris via:

🌐   www.aiccoaching.com

🄵   www.facebook.com/iris.clermont/?locale=de_DE

🄸   www.linkedin.com/in/iris-clermont-9199b17/?originalSubdomain=de

🄩   https://twitter.com/aicclermont

🄾   www.instagram.com/irisclermont